The New York Times Guide to Dining Out in New York

The New York Times

Guide to Dining Out
in New York

New 1976 edition

By John Canaday

Atheneum
New York

Library of Congress Cataloging in Publication Data
1. New York (City)—Restaurants—Directories.
I. New York Times.
II. The New York Times guide to dining out in New York.
III. Title: Guide to dining out in New York
TX907.N463 1976   647'.95747'1   75–13626
ISBN 0-689-70528-X

Contents

Publisher's Note

This new edition of *The New York Times Guide to Dining Out in New York* has been completely updated. New information—such as brunch and pre- or after-theatre specials—has been added. It indicates new telephone numbers, new addresses, revised prices, new credit card information, and hours. Comments on the restaurants' cuisine, service, and ambiance have been rewritten.

Approximately 250 establishments are covered —many of them new and not represented in the previous edition. There have been a number of deletions, as many restaurants have closed within the past year or so.

The reader is advised to check by phone regarding holiday, vacation, and weekend closings. "Closed major holidays" may mean 6 at one restaurant, 4 at another, and 5 at still another. Some establishments are closed the first week of a month which may extend until the middle of the second week due to a holiday. A very few others are noncommittal and close temporarily on very short notice, say, in case of death in a family-run business or even during a particularly severe snowstorm.

Closing times vary as well. Several 11:00 p.m.s are indicative of the last order taken at that hour and, naturally, you may stay and finish your meal. Others specifically mean the establishment's doors are locked at that time and you had better get there earlier.

7

Another updated feature we have added is a note on personal checks. This is arbitrary, at best, in that many establishments did not want this feature added—although they do accept checks from known customers. In other cases, however, acceptance is contingent on proper identification—*proper* meaning what the establishment considers so. Although we have omitted traveler's checks, as a general rule these serve as cash.

The publisher will welcome correspondence from anyone who finds inaccuracies, which will be checked and reflected in future printings.

Introduction

First off, let's make one thing clear: The restaurants reviewed in this guide, with two exceptions—La Caravelle and Sardi's—were first visited anonymously. When reservations were necessary, they were made under pseudonyms. At different times during the last couple of years I have been Rathbone, Harrington, and Wilson; Milton, Herrick, Donne, Nashe, and Cowley; Crawley, Sharp, Sedley, and Dobbin; Boone, Crockett, Travis, and Lamar, and once, for the hell of it, Gilles de Bosschère-Heim. One night at Kitcho, an excellent and very Japanese restaurant, they asked if I had a reservation and I said "Yes," which was so, but when they wanted to know what my name was, all I could say was "I can't remember." We scanned the reservation list and found I was Mr. Milton. As far as Kitcho was concerned, the Mysterious West.

The anonymity, of course, is tied to the idea that the reader who follows this guide will receive the same attention as the reviewer. For the reviewer, however, voluntary anonymity is often a little painful. There he is, free to order anything on or off the menu and in a position, if he declares himself, to be king of the roost as *The New York Times*'s restaurant man. But there he sits, unable to take advantage of anything but the cash-money in his pocket, which doesn't help even in a snob restaurant because they don't know in advance that he is going to be a heavy spender. He

9

doesn't look it. You will usually find me at the worst table in the restaurant, snuggled up against the door leading to the kitchen or the restrooms or, when possible, both.

Most restaurants that cater to a fashionable, moneyed crowd have their VIP spots and play a few favorites. That's only normal. But in some others, with "21" as the extreme example, everything depends —everything—on being known. Visiting "21" anonymously, I have been pushed off into the section called Siberia by habitués and gossip columnists, and with bigwig friends I have been enthroned at good tables. The food is the same in whatever section you sit—but so are the prices, and who goes to "21" just to eat? It's the principle of the thing. Sitting in Siberia at "21," where you see and are seen by only your fellow untouchables in this restaurant's caste system, is like paying orchestra prices for a seat in the back row of the peanut gallery. If the only thing you learn from this guide is to stay away from "21," you've already got your money's worth.

I have to admit, though, that it *is* nice to be known at a famous restaurant. I have been known at Sardi's for some 17 years now and have been treated like a prince without, let me add, ever having offered Vincent or Jimmy so much as a cigar at Christmas in appreciation. (Must remember to get around to that, one of these days.) I love the place, as my review— which see—will show. But there are not half a dozen restaurants reviewed here where I received preferential treatment, and not a single one where I received it in anticipation of a favorable review, unless there have been times when I have been recognized, without knowing it, as a restaurant reporter.

One more special thing, before we get on to general comments: When Vince Canby reviews a movie for the *Times*, and when I, in my alter ego as an art critic, write about a painting, anyone who goes to see them will see the same movie and the same painting. But you are not necessarily going to be visiting the same restaurants you read about here. Restaurants can change overnight; they are vulnerable to the whims of the chef, to the availability of the right raw food in the markets, to a waiter's headache. A big restaurant is more likely to maintain an even keel than a small one, since there are seconds-in-command to substitute for the chef in a pinch. But a small restaurant where everything depends on a single chef (I think offhand of Anastasia, La Poularde, Coriander, Paris Bistro) can go to pieces for a day if that chef is unable to work, or for keeps if he leaves. All a reviewer can do is report on the restaurant as it was when he visited it and hope for the best.

The best break you can give a restaurant reviewer is to check the date on those blown-up copies of favorable reviews that are put in the front windows. Some of them around town are as much as seven years old, and some that are much less than that have nothing to do with the restaurant in its present condition. There's one restaurant that makes me cringe every time I pass it, a thoroughly decayed eatery with my three-star review, quite deserved when the restaurant opened, exhibited as a lure.

But you can always check by peeking inside the door. Word of mouth (almost a pun here) soon determines whether a restaurant fails or succeeds after the initial impact of a favorable notice dies down. My observation has been that a restaurant where the food, price, and location are right is going to hold up well. On the pitiful side of that situation, I get letters from failing restaurants (". . . all my money is invested in this restaurant. . . ." ". . . this is my life work. . . ." "I'm pregnant") begging me to save them. Twice, the entire staff has signed the letters. ("Save our jobs.") Without a single exception, visits have shown why they are in trouble. The only honest review would have the sole virtue of a mercy blow.

A restaurant reviewer bumps into prejudices and partisanships that he never suspected existed and never manages to explain. I don't yet know what accounts for it, but I have never given a favorable review to a Turkish, Greek, or Armenian restaurant without getting a batch of letters telling me that the food was not authentic, that I was wrong all the way through, and recommending other Turkish, Greek, or Armenian restaurants to show me how wrong I was. The ones I've visited as a result have been just miserable. I still don't understand.

Such a thing as an American restaurant hardly exists in New York unless you count steak houses. There definitely is such a thing as American cuisine; I think first of fried chicken, mashed potatoes and gravy, baked ham, turkey of course, and angel food cake, apple pie and ice cream. But about 30 years ago American housewives began discovering things like boeuf bourguignon, gazpacho, and shish kebab. They also learned that the egg yolks left over from an angel food could be used to make something wonderful called zabaglione.

When they discovered herbs—that was around 1930—there was a while when you couldn't get a bowl of soup in an American home without a fistful of thyme in it. And when wine cookery began making the grade, everything was soused in red ink or cheap sherry. Now that the exaggerations have cleared up, the American palate must be just about the most versatile, even the most sophisticated, in the world. (The French palate, because of the excellence of French cuisine, may be the most subtle, but that same excellence has made the national palate the most intolerant, the most provincial.) Without any question, you can find more restaurants serving more different kinds of good food in New York than in any other city anywhere. I have noticed that the letters I get asking for the name of "a good American restaurant" come from oldsters yearning for a dinner like Mom used to make. Well, Mom doesn't cook here any more. Sis and Junior are in the kitchen whipping up a galantine of pheasant maison.

This new sophistication doesn't carry all the way through in restaurant operation, however. Let me air a personal gripe that, according to informal statistics I have gathered, is shared more widely than restaurant owners realize. I loathe, despise, and detest the way music is used in American restaurants. For a while I thought of including in this guide along with the information as to price and other essentials, a note as to whether the restaurant has a jukebox, radio, taped music, or blessed silence. When music is appropriately selected and the volume kept at a proper level, it can be a pleasant accompaniment to a meal, but this seldom happens.

It is a terrible thing, but masses of Americans have become inured to pseudo-music because they hear it all day long in elevators, in banks, in supermarkets and, alas, in their own homes. If you were to stand

13

outside a restaurant asking the diners as they exited whether there had or had not been music during the meal, half of them wouldn't be able to remember. Some restaurants turn the monster on when customers are sparse in order to alleviate a feeling of deadness. But most keep it playing all the while, with the result that the place gets noisy. As the ultimate horror, I have sat in restaurants where I was racking up a hefty check and have had to listen to radio commercials. Pay to listen to commercials? God help us all.

Now about stars:

Try not to confuse the star ratings in this guide with the Michelin system, which can give stars on the basis of food with other symbols for such things as service, style, and pleasant location. We have tried to average everything in, with the all-important factor of price counting heavily. Restaurants that didn't average out to be worthy of at least one star have been omitted—and there are surely numbers of restaurants in this city where the streets are lined with eateries, that deserve one or more stars and are unknown to us. If a restaurant doesn't appear in these pages it may mean that we omitted it purposely or that we didn't get around to it. Star ratings are being adjusted by subtraction and addition and new restaurants were being discovered and old ones dropped up to the last day of our deadline on this guide.

Judgments are necessarily subjective, and you will have to depend on individual write-ups to see how things have been balanced out in the mixture of price, food, service, ambiance, and special considerations. It will seem grotesque to many people that we have given three stars to places as dissimilar as Mario's Villa d'Este, where the food is only very good, and La

Côte Basque, where it is superb, and that we have committed the double heresy of awarding four stars to Maxwell's Plum and only three to a restaurant that makes many a gourmet swoon—Lutèce. Price is part of all that. The write-ups should explain the rest.

So we've done our best in this business of rating with stars, on the general bases of good (★), very good (★★), excellent (★★★), and extraordinary (★★★★), as follows:

★	**good**	This is a wide category, ranging from places that serve honest food at reasonable prices in pleasant surroundings, to restaurants nominally in the luxury class that may serve food of much higher quality but don't deliver what you pay for in the way of the amenities of dining in a luxury restaurant. And many kinds of restaurants in between.
★★	**very good**	As above, but more demanding.
★★★	**excellent**	Price remains a factor, but no restaurant gets a third star without something really special in the way of food or ambiance.
★★★★	**extraordinary**	Price still counts, but much less heavily than in the

other categories. All the four-star restaurants are expensive. A lunch counter serving the most delicious of hamburgers for ten cents would be the most "extraordinary" eatery in New York, but you wouldn't be dining. The four-star restaurants combine excellent or extraordinary food with agreeable or extraordinary ambiance and stylish service to an extraordinary degree.

Good luck!—which is a much more appropriate conclusion than the conventional *"Bon appétit!"*

A Note on Tipping

To all appearances there are many people who wonder about the mechanics of tipping (and tipping today is, unfortunately, by and large mechanical). As a general rule, 15 percent of the food bill is considered an adequate tip for waiters. If there is a captain, he is normally given 5 percent of the bill, and if there is a wine steward, he may be tipped $1 for each bottle served. A captain who has given very little service may be given less, or if you are pleased with what he has done for you, more. If there is only a waiter who renders service, the 15 percent should prove adequate.

In theory, of course, tipping is a voluntary act, and if the table service is conspicuously bad, the gratuity should be measured according to conscience. Restaurant-goers might keep in mind that in most restaurants where there are both waiters *and* captains, the tips are not shared. That is to say, if the diner indicates a tip on the bill or leaves a sum of money as gratuity, all of it goes to the waiter even though most of the service may have been performed by the captain. Nor is the money shared with the wine steward or bus boy. Some restaurants include lines on the check for "gratuity, waiter," and "gratuity, captain." You write in the amounts you wish and pay them with the rest of the bill. Even if space is not given for these items on the check you may write these gratuities in. Many people find it convenient to do so.

Restaurants Listed By Areas

City Hall Area (Fulton to Canal Streets)

Barclay Downtown
Berry's
Miller's
Ponte's
Suerken's

Soho (South of Houston and the Lower East Side)

Antica Roma
Ballato
The Ballroom
Bernstein-on-Essex Street

Greenwich Village (Houston to 14th Street, West of Broadway)

À Bientot
Beau Village
Captain's Table
Casey's
Charlie & Kelly
Chez Vous
The Coach House

Dardanelles Armenian Restaurant
Hunan in the Village
Inca Bar & Restaurant
Jai-Alai
La Chaumière
La Petite Ferme
Le Beau Père
Mandarin House
Mexican Gardens
One If By Land, Two If By Sea
Paris Bistro
Peter's Backyard
Portofino
Rincon de España
Sazerac House

East Village (Houston to 14th Street, East of Broadway)

Delfino's
John's

Chelsea (14th to 33rd Streets, West of Fifth Avenue)

Keen's English Chop House

14th to 33rd Streets (East of Fifth Avenue)

Balkan Armenian Restaurant
Bosphorus East
Lüchow's
Marchi's
Mr. Lee's
Mon Paris
Per Bacco!
Sal Anthony's
Z

34th to 41st Streets (West of Fifth Avenue)

Artist & Writers Restaurant
Giordano
Keen's English Chop House
Moshe Peking
Paradise Restaurant

Murray Hill (34th to 41st Streets, East of Fifth Avenue)

El Parador
Giambelli
India House East
La Maison Japonaise
Nicola Paone
Szechuan d'Or

Times Square Area (42nd to 46th Streets, West of Fifth Avenue)

Algonquin Hotel (Oak Room, Rose Room)
Barbetta
Cabaña Carioca
Café de France
Joe Allen
Kitcho
Le Chambertin
Pantheon
Rosoff's
Sardi's
Sun Luck Times Square
Xochitl

Turtle Bay (42nd to 46th Streets, East of Fifth Avenue)

Christ Cella
Crawdaddy
House of Tu
Hunam
Joe and Rose
La Bibliothèque
Nanni
Oyster Bar and Restaurant in Grand Central Terminal
Palm and Palm Too
Pietro's

Press Box Steakhouse
Saito
Scoop
Szechuan Imperial

47th to 51st Streets (West of Fifth Avenue)

Assembly Steak House
Au Tunnel (Pierre Au
    Tunnel)
Café des Sports
Charley O's Bar and Grill
Chez Napoleon
Delsomma
La Grillade
Le Alpi
Pearl's Chinese Restaurant
René Pujol
Sun Luck West

47th to 51st Streets (East of Fifth Avenue)

Billy's
Box Tree, The
Chalet Suisse
El Mirador
Fonda la Paloma
Gloucester House
Inagiku (Waldorf Astoria)
Joe and Rose

La Petite Marmite
La Toque Blanche
Le Chanteclair
Le Marmiton
Lutèce
Manny Wolf's
Onde's
Shinbashi
Shun Lee Dynasty
Tandoor
Torremolinos

52nd to 56th Streets (West of Fifth Avenue)

Angelo's Italian Restaurant
Aperitivo
Arirang House
Bangkok Cuisine
Brittany du Soir
Chez Raymond
Diogenes
French Shack, The
Georges Rey
Il Gattopardo
Italian Pavilion
La Bonne Soupe
La Caravelle
La Grillade
Larré's French Restaurant
Maneeya Thai
Orsini's
Reun-Thep

Romeo Salta
Seafare of the Aegean
"21"
Yoshi's

52nd to 56th Streets (East of Fifth Avenue)

Alicante
Billy's
Brasserie
Brazilian Pavilion
Café Argenteuil
Café Europa & La Brioche
Castilian Room
Chateau Richelieu
Four Seasons
Giovanni
Goodale's
Il Rigoletto
India Pavilion
La Côte Basque
La Grenouille
L'Aiglon
Lair, The
La Poularde
La Rotisserie
Le Cygne
Le Fontainebleau
Le Madrigal
Le Mistral
Le Perigord
Le Pont Neuf

Mario's Villa d'Este
Nippon
P.J. Clarke's
Sun Luck East
Tanpopo
Yunnan Yuan
Zapata Restaurant

Lincoln Center (57th to 72nd Street, West of Fifth Avenue)

Alfredo's of New York
Aunt Fish
Café du Centre
Frini
Genghiz Khan's Bicycle
Le Poulailler
Meson Botin
Monk's Inn, The
O Lar
Russian Tea Room

57th to 72nd Streets (East of Fifth Avenue)

Anastasia
Bruce Ho's Four Seas
Café Nicholson
Coriander
Dewey Wong
Di Anni's

Experience
Filoxenia
Gaetano's
Gavroche
Gaylord
Gian Marino
Gino
Il Valletto
Isle of Capri
Jacques'
Katja
La Cocotte
La Fleur
La Goulue
Le Bec Fin
Le Cirque
Le Colisée
Le Lavandou
Le Moal
Le Muscadet
L'Entrecôte
Le Passy
Le Perigord Park
Le Provençal
Le Steak
L'Estérel
Le Veau d'Or
Palace, The
Proof of the Pudding
Puerto Real
Quo Vadis
Roger's
Ruc
Sign of the Dove

Sun Luck Imperial
Uncle Tai's Hunan Yuan

Upper West Side (above 73rd Street, West of Fifth Avenue)

Istanbul Cuisine
Le Rabelais
P.S. 77
Ruskay's
Spring Garden (House of Siam)
Tony's Italian Kitchen

Upper East Side (above 73rd Street, East of Fifth Avenue)

Acapulco
Carrousel
Casa Brasil
Czechoslavak Praha
De Cuir
Dorrian's Red Hand
El Sombrero
Hannibal's Steak Parlor
Il Monello
La Famille
Le Boeuf à la Mode
Le Chevalier
Les Mareyeurs
Les Pleiades
Malaga
Monte Carmela

Nodeldini's
Oggi
Pancho Villa's
Parioli Romanissimo
Piro's
Purbani

Residence
Sixish
Tokubei
Tre Amici
Vašata

Four-, Three-, Two- and One-Star Restaurants

★★★★

Christ Cella
La Caravelle
Le Cygne
Maxwell's Plum
Parioli Romanissimo

★★★

Alfredo's of New York
Alicante
Arirang House
Assembly Steak House
Ballato
Bosphorus East
Box Tree, The
Café Nicholson
Casa Brasil
Casey's
Chalet Suisse
Charley O's Bar and Grill
Coriander
Dardanelles Armenian Restaurant
El Parador
Gavroche
Giambelli
Gian Marino
Giovanni
House of Tu
Hunam
Il Monello
India Pavilion
Isle of Capri
Italian Pavilion
Kitcho
La Bibliothèque
La Côte Basque
La Grenouille
La Petite Marmite
Le Colisée
Le Madrigal
Lutèce
Mandarin House
Mario's Villa d'Este
Nanni
Oyster Bar and Restaurant in Grand Central Terminal

Pearl's Chinese Restaurant
Residence
Rincon de España
Saito
Sal Anthony's
Sardi's
Tandoor
Uncle Thai's Hunan Yuan
Z

★★

À Bientot
Algonquin Hotel
Anastasia
Aperitivo
Aunt Fish
Au Tunnel (Pierre Au
    Tunnel)
Ballroom, The
Bangkok Cuisine
Barbetta
Beau Village
Berry's
Billy's
Brasserie
Brazilian Pavilion
Café Argenteuil
Café de France
Café des Sports
Café Europa & Le Brioche
Captain's Table, The

Carrousel
Charlie & Kelly
Chateau Richelieu
Chez Napoleon
Chez Vous
Coach House, The
Czechoslovak Praha
DeCuir's
Delsomma
Diogenes
Experience
Filoxenia
Fonda la Paloma
Fonda los Milagros
French Shack, The
Frini
Gaetano's
Gaylord
Georges Rey
Gino
Gloucester House
Goodale's
Il Gattopardo
Inca Bar & Restaurant
India House East
Istanbul Cuisine
Jacques'
Katja
Keen's English Chop House
La Bonne Soupe
La Cocotte
La Famille
La Fleur
La Fronde

La Goulue
La Grillade
L'Aiglon
Lair, The
La Maison Japonaise
La Petite Ferme
La Poularde
La Toque Blanche
Le Alpi
Le Beau Père
Le Boeuf à la Mode
Le Chambertin
Le Chanteclair
Le Fontainebleau
Le Mistral
Le Muscadet
L'Entrecôte
Le Perigord
Le Provençal
Les Mareyeurs
Les Pleides
L'Estérel
Manny Wolf's Chop House
Marchi's
Meson Botin
Mexican Gardens
Miller's
Mr. Lee's
Monk's Inn, The
Monte Carmela
Nicola Paone
Nippon
Nodeldini's
O Lar

Onde's
One If By Land, Two If By
    Sea
Palm and Palm Too
Pancho Villa's
Pantheon
Paris Bistro
Per Bacco!
Peter's Backyard
Pietro's
Piro's
P.J. Clarke's
Ponte's Steak House
Portofino
P.S. 77
Puerta Real
Purbani
René Pujol
Reun-Thep
Roger's
Romeo Salta
Ruc
Ruskay's
Russian Tea Room
Sazerac House
Scoop
Seafare of the Aegean
Shinbashi
Spring Garden (House of
    Siam)
Tanpopo
Tokubei
Vašata
Xochitl

Yoshi's
Yunnan Yuan
Zapata's

★

Acapulco
Angelo's Italian Restaurant
Antica Roma
Artist & Writers' Restaurant
Balkan Armenian Restaurant
Barclay Downtown
Bernstein-on-Essex Street
Brittany du Soir
Bruce Ho's Four Seas
Cabaña Carioca
Café du Centre
Castilian Room
Chez Raymond
Crawdaddy
Delfino's
Dewey Wong
Di Anni's
Dorrian's Red Hand
El Mirador
El Sombrero
Four Seasons, The
Genghiz Khan's Bicycle
Giordano
Hannibal's Steak Parlor
Hunan in the Village

Il Rigoletto
Il Valletto
Inagiku
Jai-Alai
Joe Allen
Joe and Rose
John's
La Chaumière
La Rotisserie
Larré's French Restaurant
Le Bec Fin
Le Chavalier
Le Cirque
Le Lavandou
Le Marmiton
Le Moal
Le Perigord Park
Le Pont Neuf
Le Poulailler
Le Rabelais
Le Steak
Le Veau d'Or
Lüchow's
Malaga
Mama Laura
Maneeya Thai
Mon Paris
Moshe Peking
Oggi
Orsini's
Paradise Restaurant
Press Box Steakhouse
Proof of the Pudding

Quo Vadis
Rosoff's
Shun Lee Dynasty
Sign of the Dove
Sixish
Suerken's
Sun Luck Restaurants
Szechuan d'Or
Szechuan Imperial
Tony's Italian Kitchen
Torremolinos

Tre Amici
"21"

Special Rating

$$$$ Palace, The
Because of the impossibility of averaging quality and price in this instance, the conventional star rating is omitted. See write-up.

Types of Restaurants

It is easy to define certain restaurants as French, certain others as Italian, Japanese, and so on. But there are those hybrids, usually Franco-Italian, that call themselves "Continental" and some (like Coriander, which ranges from American hamburgers to Thai delicacies) that would properly be called "Intercontinental," a vague enough term. As for "American"—what are you going to do with that gastronomical melting pot?

In the following lists we have added "Continental" to the categories given in previous editions of this guide, which saves double listing under French and Italian and sometimes elsewhere, and have included "intercontinental" cuisines in the "continental" category. "American" covers a multitude of, we hope, virtues. Even so, there are many double entries, and the reader is urged to use the lists only as points of departure for checking up on a restaurant by way of the individual write-ups. There you will find such information as the fact that Anastasia, which has a Greek listing, is Greek only on Sundays, while Casa Brasil, with a Brazilian listing, is Brazilian only on Wednesdays, and that both go continental (where they are also listed) on their other open days. Or if you chance on Seafare of the Aegean listed as Creole, to the disruption of your geographical sense, you will find that this restaurant with the Greek name includes a few Creole dishes among its specialties. And so on.

American

Algonquin Hotel
Artist & Writers' Restaurant
Assembly Steak House
Ballroom, The
Barclay Downtown
Billy's
Charlie & Kelly
Christ Cella
Coach House, The
Coriander
Frini
Hannibal's Steak Parlor
Joe Allen
Joe and Rose
La Famille
Manny Wolf's Steak House
Miller's
Nodeldini's
One If By Land, Two If By Sea
Palm and Palm Too
Peter's Backyard
P.J. Clarke's
Press Box Steakhouse
Roger's
Rosoff's
Sardi's
Scoop
Sixish
Suerken's
"21"

Armenian

Balkan Armenian Restaurant
Dardanelles Armenian Restaurant

Brazilian

Cabaña Carioca
Casa Brasil

Chinese

Bernstein-on-Essex Street
Bruce Ho's Four Seas
Dewey Wong
House of Tu
Hunam
Hunan in the Village
Mandarin House
Moshe Peking
Pearl's Chinese Restaurant
Shun Lee Dynasty
Spring Garden (House of Siam)
Sun Luck East Chinese American Restaurant
Sun Luck Imperial

Sun Luck Times Square
Sun Luck West
Szechuan d'Or
Szechuan Imperial
Uncle Tai's Hunan Yuan
Yunnan Yuan

Continental

Algonquin Hotel
Anastasia
Berry's
Box Tree, The
Brasserie
Café du Centre
Café Europa & La Brioche
Café Nicholson
Casa Brasil
Charlie & Kelly
Coriander
Di Anni's
Dorrian's Red Hand
Experience
Four Seasons
Inca Bar & Restau-
      rant
Katja
Lair, The
Le Steak
Maxwell's Plum
Mr. Lee's
Monk's Inn, The
Onde's
Proof of the Pudding

Sign of the Dove
Yoshi's

Creole

Crawdaddy
De Cuir
Sazerac House
Seafare of the Aegean

Czechoslovakian

Czechoslovak Praha
Ruc
Vašata

English and Irish

Charley O's Bar & Grill
Keen's English Chop House

French

À Bientot
Au Tunnel (Pierre Au
      Tunnel)
Beau Village
Box Tree, The
Brittany du Soir
Café Argenteuil
Café de France

Café des Sports
Café Europa & Le Brioche
Carrousel
Casey's
Chateau Richelieu
Chez Napoleon
Chez Raymond
French Shack, The
Gavroche
Georges Rey
La Bibliothèque
La Bonne Soupe
La Caravelle
La Chaumière
La Cocotte
La Côte Basque
La Fleur
La Goulue
La Grenouille
La Grillade
L'Aiglon
La Maison Japonaise
La Petite Ferme
La Petite Marmite
La Poularde
La Rotisserie
Larré's French Restaurant
La Toque Blanche
Le Bec Fin
Le Boeuf à la Mode
Le Chambertin
Le Chanteclair
Le Chevalier
Le Cirque

Le Colisée
Le Cygne
Le Fontainebleau
Le Lavandou
Le Madrigal
Le Marmiton
Le Mistral
Le Moal
Le Muscadet
L'Entrecôte
Le Passy
Le Perigord
Le Perigord Park
Le Pont Neuf
Le Poulailler
Le Provençal
Le Rabelais
Les Mareyeurs
Les Pleiades
Le Steak
L'Estérel
Le Veau d'Or
Lutèce
Mon Paris
Palace, The
Paris Bistro
P.S. 77
Quo Vadis
René Pujol
Residence

German

Lüchow's

Greek

Anastasia
Diogenes
Filoxenia
Pantheon
Paradise Restaurant
Seafare of the Aegean

Hungarian

Jacques'

Indian/Bangladesh/Pakistani

Gaylord
India House East
India Pavilion
Purbani
Tandoor

Italian

Alfredo's of New York
Angelo's Italian Res-
  taurant
Antica Roma
Aperitivo
Ballato
Barbetta
Chez Vous

Delfino's
Delsomma
Gaetano's
Giambelli
Gian Marino
Gino
Giordano
Giovanni
Il Gattopardo
Il Monello
Il Rigoletto
Il Valletto
Isle of Capri
Italian Pavilion
John's
Le Alpi
Mama Laura
Marchi's
Mario's Villa d'Este
Monte Carmela
Nanni
Nicola Paone
Oggi
Orsini's
Parioli Romanissimo
Per Bacco!
Pietro's
Piro's
Ponte's Steak House
Portofino
Romeo Salta
Sal Anthony's
Sardi's
Scoop

35

Tony's Italian Kitchen
Tre Amici

Japanese

Inagiku
Kitcho
La Maison Japonaise
Nippon
Saito
Shinbashi
Tanpopo
Tokubei
Yoshi's

Korean

Arirang House

Kosher

Bernstein-on-Essex Street
Moshe Peking

Mexican and South American

Acapulco
Brazilian Pavilion
Cabaña Carioca
Casa Brasil
El Mirador
El Parador

El Sombrero
Fonda La Paloma
Fonda Los Milagros
Frini
Mexican Gardens
Pancho Villa's
Xochitl
Zapata's

Rumanian

Le Beau Père

Russian

Russian Tea Room

Seafood

Aunt Fish
Captain's Table
Crawdaddy
Gloucester House
Goodale's
Les Mareyeurs
Nodeldini's
Oyster Bar and Restaurant
    in Grand Central Ter-
    minal
Seafare of the Aegean

Spanish

Alicante
Castilian Room

36

Jai-Alai
Malaga
Meson Botin
O Lar
Puerta Real
Rincon de España
Torremolinos

Steaks and Chops

Assembly Steak House
Barclay Downtown
Billy's
Christ Cella
Coach House, The
Hannibal's Steak Parlor
Keen's English Chop House
Le Steak
Manny Wolf's Chop House
Miller's
Palm and Palm Too
Peter's Backyard

Pietro's
P.J. Clarke's
Ponte's Steak House
Press Box Steakhouse
Suerken's

Swiss

Chalet Suisse

Thai

Bangkok Cuisine
Maneeya Thai
Reun-Thep
Spring Garden (House of
    Siam)

Turkish

Bosphorus East
Genghiz Khan's Bicycle
Istanbul Cuisine

Credit Card Information

(SEE ALSO *Publisher's Note*)

Many dining establishments honor various credit cards. For the convenience of patrons, reviews of these restaurants are followed by one or more of the following keys:

AE	*American Express*
BA	*BankAmericard*
CB	*Carte Blanche*
DC	*Diners Club*
MC	*Master Charge*
PC	*Personal Checks*

The New York Times
Guide to Dining Out in
New York

★★ A BIENTOT

9 Barrow Street (between Ave. of the Americas & Seventh Ave.)   924-3583

Move this little bistro uptown and they'd be standing in line on the sidewalk to get in at higher prices. As it is, prices are low for food lovingly prepared, whether you order à la carte or go for the complete dinner. We have had somewhat better luck, for a little more money, ordering à la carte.

The scampi Cannoise—fresh shrimp baked in a light cream sauce and delicately but unmistakably garlicked—is worthy of any restaurant in town. Among the entrées, the small steak "à la Marseillaise," with a sauce of garlic and Pernod, is also first-rate. The atmosphere is pleasantly relaxed.

Cocktails, wines and beer.

Dinner runs from $4.75 to $6.95. There is a special summer dinner, Monday thru Thursday, at $5.00.

Open 7 days a week from 6:00 p.m. till 11:30 p.m.

Closed Labor Day, Christmas Eve and Christmas Day.

Reservations recommended on weekdays, required on weekends.

No credit cards.

★ ACAPULCO

1555 Second Avenue   744-9229

The limited menu of Spanish and Mexican dishes includes nothing more unusual than chicken with rice on the Spanish side and mole poblano on the Mexican, but the preparation is good and the day we were there the portions were staggering. Acapulco's chief recommendation is an agreeable, intimate atmosphere. The bar seems to be a favorite with old patrons of the newly decorated rooms. The jukebox is likely to make a lot of noise, but the selections are Mexican, so far as we heard them, which helps.

Cocktails, wines and beer.

A la carte dishes at lunch are from about $2 to $5.85. A la carte items at dinner cost from $3.75 to $6.75.

Open 7 days a week. Open Sunday through Thursday from noon until 12:30 a.m.; Friday and Saturday until 1:00 a.m.

Reservations accepted.

Luncheon parties available, accommodating up to 72 guests.

No credit cards.   PC

★★★ ALFREDO'S OF NEW YORK
240 Central Park South   246-7050

This is one of New York's more elegant Italian restaurants, expertly operated and frequently imaginative in the cookery. The pastas are especially noteworthy, whether one of the standard types, or the exceptional ones prepared now and then (such as tortellini alla panna, ham-filled in a cream sauce). The thing to do, whether it's pasta or other dishes you're after, is to ask what's special. Fish and seafood can be remarkable, depending on what is available in the market.

Cocktails, wines and beer.

A la carte entrées at lunch cost from $5.00 to $8.50, Monday through Friday. Dinner—Monday through Saturday—is about $6.50 to $12.00.

Open from noon till 11:00 p.m.; Saturday from 5:00 p.m. till midnight.

Closed Saturday for lunch and all day Sunday.

Reservations recommended.

AE   DC   MC

44

★★ ALGONQUIN HOTEL

59 West 44th Street   *687-4400*

We haven't included many hotel dining rooms in this guide, but what would our city be without the Algonquin? Both the Rose Room and the Oak Room—the latter especially popular with publishers and people like that at lunch—provide ambiances not quite like anything else in New York, although sometimes you have to forgive imperfections of service. Then too, there's the lobby, where you can sit and have drinks beforehand or while waiting for a table. (Pleasant bar, too, on the other side of the entrance.) The after-theatre buffet is the most enjoyable in town. Ah, Algonquin!

Cocktails, wines and beer.

All dishes are à la carte, with main courses at midday from about $5.25 to $12.50; in the evening, from about $7.50 to $12.50. The after-theatre menu is from $5.25 to $8.75.

Open from noon to 9:30 p.m. daily; closed Sunday for dinner only. Closed for dinner only on Christmas, July 4th, Labor Day and Thanksgiving. Brunch is served on Sunday from noon to 2:15 p.m. A traditional supper buffet is served Monday through Saturday from 9:30 p.m. to 12:30 a.m.

Reservations recommended.

AE BA CB DC MC

★★★ ALICANTE

251 East 53rd Street   *421-5360*

Opening late in 1974, Alicante immediately established itself as an efficiently operated restaurant with an unusual number of Spanish dishes not frequently found in American restaurants. Also, the quarters are spacious enough so that tables are not crowded together. An anteroom near the bar and an alcove off the main room are cozier, if that's your preference.

Alicante's gazpachillo campero was something new to us, a cold white soup with a base of oil and cream with a touch of tomato, the texture being something like vichyssoise. In this are sprinklings, according to how you like it, of chopped cucumber, green pepper, onion, and hard-boiled egg white. Among other good openers for a meal are shrimps Alicante, fresh and delicate in a spicy sauce; steamed mussels Valenciana in a beautiful broth, and beef and chicken liver skewers. An acquaintance who likes tripe (which we don't) pronounced tripe Madrileña excellent.

Among entrées, breast of chicken Cantabric was accompanied by a small lobster tail split and grilled, a very good combination. Several dishes have Mexican-sounding names but aren't at all Mexican. Beef and chicken tacos, for instance, although wrapped in corn pancakes something like tortillas, are more like a Spanish version of French crêpes. Lobster enchilada ("enchilada" meaning, literally, "chili-peppered") is doubly misleading. This really delicious dish is made up of sweet green and red peppers, sautéed and served over sections of lobster tail, with rice.

And, of course, there's paella, which is prepared in line with Alicante's general excellence.

Cocktails, wines and beer.

All dishes are à la carte, with main courses at midday from about $3.50 to $7.50; in the evening, from about $4.25 to $9.50.

Open Monday through Thursday from noon till 11:00 p.m.; Friday and Saturday till midnight. Closed Sunday.

Closed New Year's Day, July 4th, Labor Day, Thanksgiving and Christmas.

46

Reservations accepted.
AE   MC

★★ ANASTASIA

1384 First Avenue (at 74th Street)   535-9722

   With simple fare at lunch, running to sandwiches and omelets, Anastasia blooms at dinner. It's a very personal kitchen and, for that matter, a very personal dining room, informal but not bohemian. The menu varies, and so, to some extent, does the excellence of the preparation, as is natural in what we have already called a very personal kitchen. But this is a lovely little restaurant.

   We have been delighted at different visits with hors d'oeuvre such as marinated herbed shrimp, and a simple, hearty, and full-flavored vegetable soup. Salads? This is the kind of restaurant that would close down for a period of purification if a head of iceberg lettuce got into the kitchen by malchance. Desserts? We know a man who ate three crème brulées in a row at Anastasia's.

   Mussel stew (a generous stack in a bath of deliciously seasoned thin broth), filet of sole Ambassador (poached, with a delicate creamy sauce), and stuffed breast of lamb have all made us happy that we happened to hit Anastasia's on nights when they were available.

   On Sundays, Anastasia herself, who is usually caring for things in the dining room, takes over in the kitchen and prepares Greek dishes. Although we haven't had an opportunity to sample this Only-on-Sundays cuisine, we'd trust it to be first-rate.

   A few nights ago we passed Anastasia's to look through the window and saw that it was full. A man standing nearby said to his companion, "They must be doing something right. It's like this all the time," which is a good summary of Anastasia's virtues.

Wines and beer.

All dinner dishes are à la carte and cost from $2.50 to $6.50.

Open for dinner only: Tuesday, Wednesday & Thursday 6:00–11:00 p.m.; Friday & Saturday 6:00 to midnight; Sunday 5:00–11:00 p.m. Closed Sunday for lunch and all day Monday.

Reservations not accepted.

No credit cards.

★ ANGELO'S ITALIAN RESTAURANT

859 Ninth Avenue (at 55th Street)   CO 5-9081

This is the simplest restaurant included in this guide and probably (prices keep changing everywhere) the least expensive for the quantity of food you get. Whether or not eating here can be called dining depends on what you demand in the way of décor and service. But this Angelo's (there are three others in the telephone book, unrelated) has an enthusiastic following among professional people who can afford to eat wherever they want to and know good food wherever they find it. This food is very Italian, including pizza, and although we feel it is no better than the food in a couple of dozen other small Italian restaurants not listed here, one thing is certain: If there is any restaurant in New York that serves larger portions, we haven't run across it.

Cocktails, wines and beer.

All dishes are à la carte and begin at $2.00.

Open from 11:30 to midnight.

Open 7 days a week.

Reservations are recommended.

No credit cards.

48

★ ANTICA ROMA

40 Mulberry Street   *267-2242*

This is an intimate spot that has endeared itself to a clientele that keeps it full most nights. The atmosphere, definitely informal, is one of happy family unity between kitchen and dining room. The pastas are homemade, and Italophiles especially recommend the gnocchi (small poached dumplings). We're not fond of gnocchi, but agree that at Antica Roma they are prepared with the light touch that is imperative if they aren't to turn soggy.

Standard dishes are carefully prepared. A self-indulgent dinner for two with a full bottle of good wine can run up to $30, but with a little self-control you can cut the figure in half.

Cocktails, wines and beer.

A la carte entrées at lunch cost from about $3.25 to $8.25. A la carte dinners are from $3.50 to $8.50. There is a special dinner for two for $17.00.

Open from noon to midnight.

Closed Thanksgiving, Christmas and New Year's Day.

Reservations are recommended at lunch, accepted at dinner.

AE   DC   MC

★★ APERITIVO

29 West 56th Street   *765-5155*

When a restaurant totally without snob value stays popular for as long as Aperitivo has, it's got to be the food. It's very Italian—strong tomato sauces, but made in the kitchen, not bought by the gallon can. We have one small objection to the service. It is not exactly ungracious, yet it is abrupt, and somewhat rushed. Perhaps only in the interest of taking care of us properly, the captain didn't give us all the time we

49

needed for a leisurely inspection of the menu. When he came around for the third time, rather insistently, we ordered.

But it's a very satisfying restaurant in general. A nice touch is that your cheese is grated directly onto your dish from a big wedge, assuring undiminished flavor.

As an unimportant side issue, the paintings all over the walls are just about the worst, and the most over-framed, of any restaurant we know. They are an appropriate part, however, of the elaborate décor, which has an appealingly innocent gaudiness.

Cocktails, wines and beer.

All dishes are à la carte and cost from about $6.50 to $10.00.

Open from noon till 10:30 p.m. Monday through Friday; from 5:30 p.m. till 11:00 p.m. on Saturday. Closed Saturday for lunch and all day Sunday.

Closed all major holidays.

Reservations recommended.

AE   BA   DC

★★★ ARIRANG HOUSE
28 West 56th Street   LT *1-9698 and* LT *1-9699*

This restaurant is enthusiastically recommended on several scores beside the food, which also happens to be first-rate. The service is excellent, and if it weren't you would excuse any flaws because the waitresses, floating around in their Korean dress, are the loveliest flock of creatures imaginable in this city where charming exotics come 13 to the dozen. The restaurant is comfortable, your reception friendly, and the price reasonable for all you get.

Not being well acquainted with Korean cuisine we usually tell the head man or waitress what we would like in a general way—fish, chicken, beef, or seafood, spicy, bland, or medium—and take what comes. Special dishes can be prepared any time with a little advance notice. We once had a fine meal for four people, ordered 48 hours in advance, for only $10 a person, wine extra. Prices are probably higher by now for a similar meal.

To give you an idea of what to expect, we remember a sweet-and-sour chicken, more Indonesian than Chinese in suggestion, with lots of pineapple; pul koki, described as "prime thinly sliced sirloin in a marinade of unique and exotic spices unknown to Occidentals," which, although not grilled at the table as promised on the menu, was so good that one of our guests broke a chopstick in his gluttony; sam hapcho, consisting of shrimp, abalone, sirloin tips, carrots, water chestnuts, seaweed, celery, and mushrooms in sweet and sour wine sauce, that arrived looking like a bouquet; and an appetizer, kujol pan, combining marinated beef finely chopped with bean sprouts and other vegetables, wrapped in a tissue-thin pancake collar. All very exotic, yet not shocking to the Occidental palate.

Cocktails, wines and beer.

A la carte luncheons are priced from about $2.50 to $5.25; complete lunch is about $4.25. Complete dinners cost $8.50 to $8.95, with à la carte dishes from about $4.00 to $6.50.

Open from noon to 10:30 p.m. Closed all day Sunday and Saturday for lunch.

Closed New Year's Day.

Reservations accepted.

AE   CB   DC   MC

★ ARTIST & WRITERS' RESTAURANT
213 West 40th Street   LO *3-2424*

Not at all arty, the Artist & Writers' Restaurant, generally called Bleak's by the savvy, is a cross between a chophouse and a rathskeller. It has a great bar, a somewhat hermetic group of dining rooms, and an enthusiastic clientele that is now more midtown business than artistic and literary. Back in the days when there was a *Herald Tribune,* this restaurant (and, above all, bar) would have been voted the favorite of favorites by journalists from across the street. *New York Times* men were tolerated as well. The food is very hearty, the service very no-nonsense. Artist & Writers has as much special personality as any restaurant in New York.

Cocktails, wines and beer.

All dishes are à la carte and cost from $4.50 to $8.25.

Open Monday through Friday from 11:30 to 9:15 p.m. Closed Saturday and Sunday.

Closed all major holidays.

Reservations recommended at lunch; not necessary for dinner.

All major credit cards.

★★★ ASSEMBLY STEAK HOUSE
16 West 51st Street   *581-3580*

If you like a big, busy restaurant (nice for a change) where the food is more notable for honesty than subtlety and the service is more efficient than elegant, you should like the Assembly Steak House. Not that this is one of those steak houses that go in aggressively for a meat-and-potatoes-and-no-nonsense atmosphere, with sawdust on the floor and sleeve garters on the waiters. On the contrary, the Assembly's quarters are rather elaborately decorated, with lots of red stuff around, and well-arranged bouquets of dried grasses and artificial flowers spotted effectively here and there. But it remains a hearty rather than a fashionable restaurant.

In addition to the standard steak-house menu, they have some specialties. There's a sherried black bean soup, although "beans" would be more accurate than "bean soup," since the big bowl of whole beans is barely covered with an excellently flavored juice.

Also, the Assembly has "revived," as they put it, the porterhouse steak, a choice cut from the chateaubriand and filet section of the carcass. Mixed green salad comes with this (as it does with all entrées) and it is a good idea to add Assembly German fried potatoes —exactly as they should be, very homey, with a few fried black and hard.

All told, though, the prize entrée is baked filet of sole Assembly. The delicate fish is wrapped around a crabmeat stuffing.

An interesting variation on the usual wine list is that in this extensive one (114 choices), certain selections are starred as being "above average quality and moderately priced." "Moderately" begins at $5.00 for a white Beaujolais and goes up to $70.00 for a Château Lafite-Rothschild, Pauillac, 1964. Just shows how relative "moderate" can be.

Cocktails, wines and beer.

At lunch, à la carte dishes cost from about $4.95 to $7.95. There is a pre–theatre roast prime rib dinner at $10.95. A la carte entrées at dinner cost from $6.25 to $11.95.

Open Monday through Saturday from 11:30 to 10:30 p.m. Closed Sunday.

Closed all major holidays.

Reservations recommended.
Parties and catered affairs can be arranged.
AE BA CB DC MC

★★ AUNT FISH
1 Lincoln Plaza (63rd Street and Broadway)   799-7200
    If you want fish before or after the ballet, the opera, or the Philharmonic, this is your place. A little crowded, maybe, but the kitchen holds to a good level and the service is brisk.
Cocktails, wines and beer.
All dishes are à la carte, with main courses at midday from about $3.95 to $8.00; in the evening, from about $5.75 to $14.00. There is an after-theatre special supper menu from $3.95 to $8.00.
Open 7 days a week.
Reservations recommended.
There is live music on Sunday from 3:00 to 5:00 p.m.
All major credit cards.

★★ AU TUNNEL (formerly PIERRE AU TUNNEL)
306 West 48th Street   582-2166
    Low prices account for this restaurant's second star. Otherwise it would be a single for honest French cooking and cheerful service in rather crowded quarters. We have eaten here at intervals widely spaced over 17 years and can't see that anything ever changes—which is fine, when the formula is good.
Cocktails, wines and beer.
At lunch, à la carte dishes cost from about $3.50 to $5.75. Table d'hôte dinners are from $6.25 to $8.75.
Open Monday through Saturday, except summer, from noon to 11:30 p.m.

54

Closed all day Sunday and for Saturday lunch May to September.

Closed all major holidays.

Reservations accepted at lunch; recommended for parties of three or more for dinner.

AE

★ BALKAN ARMENIAN RESTAURANT
129 East 27th Street   689-7925

Although vehemently Armenian in spirit, this good restaurant makes a few concessions to overlappings with Middle Eastern cuisine in general, and somehow manages to hold to about as low a price level as is possible for plentiful food in a New York eatery without sacrificing quality. A good test of a restaurant that has been around for a number of years is the consistency of patronage. With its tables in steady demand, Balkan Armenian passes with high marks.

Cocktails, wines and beer.

A la carte entrées at lunch are from $3.50 to $5.50. A la carte entrées at dinner are from $4.00 to $6.50; 7-course table d'hôte is from $7.25 to $9.75.

Open Monday through Thursday from noon till 9:00 p.m.; noon to 9:30 p.m. on Friday and 4:30 to 10:30 Saturday. Closed Saturday for lunch and all day Sunday.

Closed major holidays and the first two weeks of July.

Reservations recommended.

AE   DC   MC

★★★ BALLATO
55 East Houston Street   CA 6-9683

This 12-table restaurant on the extreme northern border of SoHo achieves a paradoxical elegance in its spare, immaculate, low-profiled way and is a

favorite with artists, writers, and critics who have
made the grade uptown, a demanding clientele that
likes a relaxed atmosphere. John Ballato—a senior citi-
zen who resembles photographs of Henri Matisse at
the same age—is proud of his restaurant and his clientele. For that matter, the rest of the staff go about their
jobs as if the restaurant were going to survive or per-
ish on the strength of your response to the dish being
prepared and served at the moment.

The cuisine is largely North Italian. I like to take
Mr. Ballato's suggestion as to what might be particularly good that night. Remember one thing: If you
aren't on time for your reservation, it won't be held
for you longer than ten or fifteen minutes.

Wines and beer.

*All dishes are à la carte and cost from about $4.75 to $10.00
for both lunch and dinner.*

Open from noon to 9:00 p.m. Monday to Saturday.

Closed Sunday.

Reservations recommended at lunch; required at dinner.

No credit cards.

★★ BALLROOM, THE

458 West Broadway (between Houston and Prince Streets)
473-9367

The Ballroom is a pretty place, the food is very
good indeed, and the price is right. When things are
going smoothly, it well deserves a third star, but it can
panic in a pinch, and even under normal circumstances the amateur waiters aren't always up to
scratch. But don't let this keep you away. The risk is
worth taking.

The Ballroom was the first restaurant to recognize
that SoHo had outgrown its beards-and-blue-jeans

bohemianism and had developed its own kind of elegance, achieved in lofts and art galleries with a broom, a do-it-yourself manual, and gallons of white paint. The Ballroom added hanging plants and lit globes that seem to float at different levels below the ceiling, and borders of tiny clear lights for an interior that can hold its own against more conventionally flossy places.

A recommended specialty is pillow of chicken, pieces of breast cooked with mushrooms in wine and wrapped in flaky pastry. It comes in looking like an enormous Danish and is excellent. The Japanese beef with vegetables, the beef strips lightly marinated and quick fried with onions, celery, scallions, broccoli, and mushrooms, would be hard to beat in either Tokyo or New York.

There is entertainment around 10 or 10:30, but we haven't stayed for it, hence can't report.

Cocktails, wines and beer.

At lunch, à la carte dishes cost from about $2.00 to $4.00. At dinner, à la carte dishes cost from about $2.50 to $7.00. Sunday brunch is from $3.50 to $4.50 and includes one drink and coffee.

Closed for lunch on Monday. Open all other times, excluding August lunch, from noon to midnight; later on Friday & Saturday nights. Sunday brunch is from 1:00–4:30 p.m.

Reservations recommended for dinner on weekends.

There is cabaret entertainment at 10:30 every night and at 10:30 and midnight on Friday and Saturday.

No credit cards.

★★ BANGKOK CUISINE

885 Eighth Avenue (between 52nd and 53rd Streets)
581-6370

What Bangkok Cuisine doesn't offer in style it makes up in the authenticity of the Thai dishes, including low-cost noodles that are a full meal. One that we tried, called pad Thai rice stick noodle, combined shrimp, bits of tender white fish, bean sprouts, and assorted spices.

We can recommend sliced hot-and-sour beef with lemon grass, "lemon grass" being a Thai herb flavoring; beef curry, although "curry" in Thai cuisine means a thick peanut sauce rather than an Indian combination of spices; and fried whole fish topped with ginger, bamboo shoots, and dried mushrooms.

This is a Thai-Vietnamese neighborhood and you can choose between three restaurants—this one and, nearby, Maneeya Thai and Reun Thep, which see.

Wines and beer.

All dishes are à la carte, with main courses at midday from about $1.95 to $2.95; in the evening, from about $2.95 to $5.95.

Closed for lunch on Sunday. Open all other days from 11:00 to midnight.

Sunday open 5:00 to midnight.

Open all year, except Sunday lunch.

Reservations required for dinner, excluding holidays.

AE   DC

★ BARBETTA

321 West 46th Street   CI 6-9171

If looks would do it, Barbetta's would be right up there in the top bracket of New York restaurants, since this is one of the handsomest dining rooms in the city, with a delightful garden that is open in good weather. For this reason it continues to flourish, and even to remain many people's favorite restaurant in spite of uneven food (the best is excellent, the worst leaves plenty to be desired) and notoriously bad service. Out in the garden you sometimes have to run up a storm signal to get a waiter's attention. Even so, the place is so pretty that, forewarned, a visitor to New York could do much worse than to spend an evening there.

Cocktails, wines and beer.

Table d'hôte lunch is from $8.25 up. Pretheatre dinner is $13.50. The à la carte menu at dinner is from $8.25 up.

Open Monday through Saturday from noon until midnight.

Pretheatre dinner is from 5:00 p.m. until 7:00 p.m.

Closed Sunday, July 4th, Labor Day, Thanksgiving, Christmas and New Year's Day. Call for summer vacation closing.

Reservations recommended.

Party and banquet facilities available for up to 250 guests. Outdoor garden for alfresco dining. Fashion show luncheon on Wednesdays. Baroque music on Thursday and Friday from 8:30 to 11:30 p.m. Barbera and Grigndino wine from family vineyards in Fubine, Monferrato, in the region of Piemonte, Italy.

AE   CB   DC   MC

★ BARCLAY DOWNTOWN
57 Murray Street   349-0508

Like other restaurants serving the City Hall neighborhood, Barclay Downtown runs to steaks and seafood in its extensive menu and cultivates a pubby personality. Service is brisk and friendly and the bar is particularly attractive. As a slightly exotic specialty,

59

they are proud of their abalone steak, flown in from the West Coast. Abalone not being our dish of tea, we haven't tried it, but judging from other dishes we have sampled here, it is likely to be good.

We particularly liked Barclay's baked clams arregante—their spelling—which were pungently herbed and so deliciously garlicked that we were an offense around the house for the next 24 hours. These were really as good as we've ever had anywhere in the baked-clam division.

Potato pancakes with apple sauce and green salad were first-rate in their honest, straightforward way—the *only* way for a genuine potato pancake. Broiled pork chops were pleasingly hefty and accompanied by potatoes, vegetable, and salad. Broiled fresh salmon trout, accompanied by the same, was also satisfactory.

Cocktails, wines and beer.

At lunch and dinner à la carte dishes cost from about $2.95 to $7.95.

Open Monday through Friday from 11:00 a.m. to 8:00 p.m. Closed Saturday and Sunday and all major holidays.

AE BA CB DC MC PC

★★ BEAU VILLAGE
49 Charles Street (corner of West 4th Street)   741-2523
This restaurant had a rude shock when it opened about three years ago and discovered that its proximity to a church prohibited it by law from selling liquor. A deserted bar greets you upon entrance, a sad spectacle. Otherwise it's a most agreeable spot, and delivery from a nearby liquor store is prompt, if you want wine.

We have had very good food here, including mushrooms Provençale, pickled with onion, celery, and green pepper, a fine pepper steak, and an unusual calf's liver dish, with a sweetish sauce including grapes. It's a quiet place, very good for a leisurely meal with someone you enjoy talking to.

No alcoholic beverages; bring your own bottle.

Open for dinner only with à la carte entrées from $3.95 to $8.50.

Open Monday through Saturday from 6:00 to 11:30 p.m. Closed Sunday.

Closed Sunday and all major holidays.

Reservations recommended.

BA   MC

★ BERNSTEIN-ON-ESSEX STREET

135 Essex Street   GR *3-3900*

Bernstein's approximation of real Chinese food within kosher restrictions is a triumph of culinary ingenuity over dietary laws. The supervision of Rabbi Samuel Walkin guarantees that your moo-goo-gai-pen is 100 percent kosher, and your palate would hardly suspect that it is not 100 percent Chinese.

Pork, a Chinese staple, is forbidden to orthodox Jews while veal is nonexistent in true Chinese cookery, but Bernstein-on-Essex successfully substitutes veal for pork—sweet and pungent veal instead of sweet and pungent pork, for instance. The restriction against shellfish knocks out a lengthy category of Chinese delicacies that aren't quite made up for by "Another Bernstein First! Oriental franks! Franks cut in chunks with sweet sour sauce garnished with pineapple chunks and green peppers topped with Chinese vermicelli."

The chief difference from the best Chinese cuisine, apparent in most of the dishes we tried, was their heaviness. The best thing was the vegetables. Plentiful and typically Chinese, they were wonderfully fresh and barely cooked, in the best Chinese tradition.

Like a Chinese restaurant in Chinatown, Bernstein-on-Essex is totally unglamorous—a bare room with simple tables.

Wines and beer.

All dishes are à la carte, with main courses at midday from about $1.75; in the evening, from about $3.50.

Closed Friday at sundown until Saturday at sundown. Open Sunday through Thursday until 1:00 a.m., Saturday until 3:00 a.m.

Closed all Jewish holidays.

Reservations accepted.

No credit cards.

★★ BERRY'S

180 Spring Street (at Thompson Street)   226-4394

Berry's is less a restaurant than a cafe along European lines, where they also serve meals. The room is dominated by one of the finest old mahogany bars left in this city, and it stays in business until 4 a.m. after the kitchen closes down around 11. Tables are small and close together. When Berry's is full, "chummy" is an inadequate adjective.

We had one unhappy experience at Berry's: steak tartare. The beef just wasn't good enough to begin with. But otherwise we've found the kitchen fine and often imaginative. Only a few dishes are offered per night. These are chalked up on a blackboard. We have hit nights when the filet of sole, roast lamb, broiled shrimp, and breast of chicken have been excellent. Also, we were delighted to find vegetables lightly cooked, and rice (a real test) that hit just the right level between moist and dry. We feel safe in recommending this spot if you will bear in mind that it is extremely informal.

Cocktails, wines and beer.

Dinner is à la carte, with main courses from about $3.95 to $5.75. Snacks are $1.50 to $2.25. Saturday and Sunday brunch is from $2.50 to $3.00.

Open for dinner only. Open weekdays from 6:00 to 11:30 p.m.; weekends from 6:00 to midnight. Open Saturday and Sunday from noon to midnight. Saturday and Sunday brunch from noon to 3:00 p.m. Kitchen is open till 4:00 a.m. with snacks. Snacks before and after dinner and at the bar at all times: 4 p.m. to 4 a.m. Tues.-Fri.; noon to 4:00 a.m. Sat. & Sun.

Closed Monday and Christmas.

No credit cards.

★★ BILLY'S

948 First Avenue (between 52nd and 53rd Streets)
355-8920

This famous little steak house, established in 1870, had to move from its former location when the building was razed in 1967, but managed to do a pretty good job of re-creating itself with the old fixtures in its new quarters. It's a warm, comfortable pub with a warm, comfortable kind of clientele, and over the 16 years that we have been eating there, we have yet to be disappointed.

There are steaks, pork chops (these broiled black on the outside, still succulent on the inside), chicken, and fish, as well as a few side dishes. Sometimes, bay scallops. All entrées come with potatoes (baked or french fried) and a generous dish of cole slaw.

Cocktails, wines and beer.

63

All dishes are à la carte, with main courses at midday from about $2 to $5; in the evening, from about $4.95 to $11.75.

Open daily, except July & August, from noon to midnight. Closed Saturdays July and August.

Closed New Year's Day, Memorial Day, July 4th, Labor Day, Thanksgiving and Christmas.

Reservations recommended at dinner.

AE   CB   DC   MC

★★★ BOSPHORUS EAST

121 Lexington Avenue (at 28th Street)   679-8370

Whether Bosphorus East is Turkish or Armenian seems to be a moot point among purists. It calls itself Turkish and that is all right with us, the main point being that it is a charming room serving excellent food. Opening notices made much of its being operated by a former belly dancer, a rather ambiguous gastronomical allure, but when a Turkish foreign correspondent recommended it we went there quickly.

If you have the idea that all Middle Eastern food is oily and violently flavored, you can see how wrong you are with an order of hunkar begendi—chunks of tender lamb on a bed of eggplant purée. Scara koefte (ground meat cakes with onions) are accompanied by a delicious lightly grilled half green pepper and a grilled half tomato, all on a bed of lettuce.

As an appetizer we liked midia dolma, mussels in shells stuffed with rice flavored with chopped onions, pignolia nuts, currants, and spices, served cold. Also, with whatever you are having, try a side order of djajek, a mixture of yogurt, cucumbers, garlic, and parsley.

Some of those glittering fabrics draped on the walls

64

of Bosphorus East are belly dancer's skirts, helping to make this a really pretty room.

Wines and beer.

All dishes are à la carte, with main courses at midday from about $3.00 to $6.00; in the evening, from about $3.50 to $6.50.

Open Tuesday through Sunday from noon to 11:00 p.m. Closed Monday.

Reservations accepted at lunch, recommended at dinner. AE DC MC

★★★ BOX TREE, THE
242 East 50th Street (between Second and Third Avenues) 758-8320

This very small restaurant, a recent arrival, well deserves the popularity that makes a table virtually impossible to get without a reservation well in advance. The space, tiny to begin with, is divided into two rooms and decorated to the hilt in a rather precious way—stained-glass screens rescued from some demolished turn-of-the-century mansion, a pannier of polished apples on the floor (sometimes to the inconvenience of the waiters), bouquets of calla lilies, and the like. Everybody gets a rosebud with his napkin and you get another with your check.

Except for one unfortunate experience with a piece of mushy liver (perfection another time), we have found the food excellent. It is obviously carefully prepared individual dish by individual dish. They try, with success, to make interesting variations on familiar themes—for instance, Bayonne ham and pear for an appetizer instead of the usual prosciutto and melon, and a sorrel sauce with fresh salmon. However, there isn't much point in describing individual dishes here, since the menu changes. Add wine and service charges

65

to the prices listed and you'll see that it isn't inexpensive, but if you feel like spending the money, The Box Tree will give you full value for it.

Apéritifs, wines and beer.

Complete luncheons are priced from about $9.50 to $12.50.
Complete dinner from $16.50 to $19.50.

Open Monday through Saturday from 12:30 until 11:00 p.m.
Closed Sunday and all major holidays.

Reservations required.

No credit cards.

★★ BRASSERIE

100 East 53rd Street   751-4840

You can walk into the Brasserie any time of the day or night—it's open 24 hours out of the 24—and except in the wee-est and smallest hours, choose from a menu that seems to have set out to represent every national cuisine with at least one dish. The atmosphere is businesslike and the service is efficient. In other words, not a place devoted to anything you could call gracious dining, but admirable in its straightforward way. And always there when you need it.

Cocktails, wines and beer.

All dishes are à la carte, with main courses at midday from about $4.75 and up; in the evening, from about $6.85 and up. A la carte brunch at other times is about $4.50.

Open 7 days a week, 24 hours. Saturday and Sunday brunch from 11:00 a.m. until 5:00 p.m.

No reservations.

AE   BA   CB   DC   MC

★★ BRAZILIAN PAVILION

141 East 52nd Street   PL *8-8129*

After a couple of meals at the Brazilian Pavilion, Manhattan's closest thing to a classy restaurant of its national type, you will begin to believe that the Brazilians are a race apart, transformed from their Portuguese origins by something or other—Amazon water?—that has given them appetites and digestive capacities beyond those of other mortal men. Like Mexican cuisine, Brazilian is a colonial hybrid, but the two have little in common. There's a lot of marinating, a love for cooking things black or dying them black in a tincture of black bean sauce, various degrees of violence in things like sausages and more curious concoctions, and starchy manioc instead of Mexican cornmeal. It's powerful stuff, but with Brazilian restaurants on the increase in New York, the natives in these parts may grow to like it in the way they have come around in hordes to a taste for even more exotic Japanese food. The Brazilian Pavilion should be tried by anyone with any sense of adventure in eating, preferably after a day's fasting.

Cocktails, wines and beer.

All dishes are à la carte, with entrées at midday and dinner from about $2.25 to $5.95.

Open Monday through Saturday from noon until 10:00 p.m.

Closed Sunday.

Reservations recommended.

BA   MC

★ BRITTANY DU SOIR

800 Ninth Avenue (at 53rd Street)   CO 5-4820 and CI 7-9566

This little bistro, just far enough away from the center of things to have a secluded air about it, has learned the secret of restaurant longevity: good food at moderate prices. Very French. And really not out-of-the-way at all.

Cocktails, wines and beer.

All dishes are à la carte, with main courses at midday from about $3.50 to $7.00; in the evening, from about $5.00 to $9.00.

Open Monday through Thursday from noon to 10:30 p.m.; Friday and Saturday until 11:15 p.m.

Closed Sunday and all major holidays.

Reservations accepted.

No credit cards.

★ BRUCE HO'S FOUR SEAS

116 East 57th Street   421-4292 and PL 3-2610

Any restaurant with a menu describing chow mein as a "classic" dish is going to be rejected on sight by purists, even if they don't notice the Po-Hai gimlet, a cocktail "Confucius couldn't resist." These objections hold right down the line at Bruce Ho's, but the food is tasty. It's also rather expensive for a Chinese restaurant—but then, we've already said this isn't really one. Atmosphere? Strictly New York, including barflies. We considered a second star. Your play.

Cocktails, wines and beer.

Complete luncheons with soup and dessert are from $3.25 to $8.75. A la carte dinners are from $3.25 to $9.75. There is a special after-theatre Bot Bo platter for two, including 2 drinks, for $10.00.

Open daily from noon until midnight.

68

Closed July 4th weekend, Thanksgiving and Christmas.
Reservations recommended.
AE BA CB DC

★ CABANA CARIOCA

123 West 45th Street   582-8088

Never having eaten in a Brazilian country inn, we can't vouch for any resemblance between a typical one and this steamy little place at the top of an unpromising stairway, but if it isn't like Brazil, it isn't quite like anything else in New York either. With veritable vats of good food at low prices, it is probably the noisiest restaurant this side of Rio, what with its uninhibited clientele and a radio tuned at full blast to a Spanish-speaking station.

Feijoada completa, described on the menu as the national dish of Brazil, is a stew of various meats, all blackened in their bath of black beans. We recognized beef, chicken, and sausage and suspected pork and rabbit in the mixture, and wouldn't have been surprised at boa constrictor. Like other entrées, this comes with more black beans (delicious), a mountain of rice (perfectly cooked), home-fried potatoes (excellent), and chopped lettuce salad (indifferent).

Another regional specialty is steak with fried egg on top. Steak gaucho style is topped with a relish of freshly chopped onions, green pepper, and tomato in vinegar and a hint of Tabasco. Portuguese omelet is an enormous dry disk, chock-a-block with onions and sausage, ringed with those fried potatoes.

Fairly rough, but a trencherman's dream, Cabaña Carioca is right smack dab in the center of the theater district. Very convenient, if you can keep awake afterwards during the show.

Cocktails, wines and beer.
All dishes are à la carte and cost from about $2.05 to $5.45.
Open 7 days a week from noon to 11:00 p.m.
Reservations recommended at both lunch and dinner.
No credit cards.

★★ CAFE ARGENTEUIL

253 East 52nd Street   PL *3-9273*

Once a moderately expensive relaxed restaurant of great charm, Café Argenteuil now aspires to culinary grandeur and beautiful-people clientele —and comes close to making the grade. A specialty, bass en croûte stuffed with lobster mousse, is among the excellent haute-cuisine numbers. But in spite of the fact that we were recognized on our last visit as a restaurant reviewer, the waiters were unable to avoid jostling our shoulders as they passed by in the narrow aisles of a crowded room. The atmosphere was a bit frantic, which doesn't go with good food and high prices.

Cocktails, wines and beer.
Table d'hôte lunch costs from about $7.95 to $14.95. Dinners are à la carte, with main courses from about $10.95 to $15.95.
Open from noon to 10:30 Monday through Friday; 11:00 p.m. on Saturday.
Closed Saturday for lunch and all day Sunday.
Reservations recommended for lunch and dinner.
AE CB DC MC

★★ CAFE DE FRANCE

330 West 46th Street,   *265-8927*

Here's a very agreeable place, making no attempt at spectacular cookery but turning out consistently superior dishes. The ambience is casual but the service is efficient. Everything tastes good, you feel welcome (odd that this should be listed as an attraction in a restaurant, but in New York you don't always), and a visit doesn't bankrupt you.

Cocktails, wines and beer.

At lunch, à la carte dishes are from $3.50 to $4.50. Table d'hôte dinner is from $6.75 to $10.50.

Open Monday through Thursday from noon until 10:30; Friday and Saturday until 11:30 p.m.

Closed Sunday and all major holidays.

Reservations accepted at lunch; recommended at dinner.

AE   BA   DC   MC

★★ CAFE DES SPORTS

329 West 51st Street   581-1283

Genuinely French in an unassuming, friendly way, and blessed with a quiet, relaxed clientele, the Café des Sports is an exceptionally pleasant little spot where you expect, and find, the standard boeuf bourguignon and coq au vin as staples. But they have also prepared for us a very good veal à la crème with mushrooms. If you allow yourself an extra few minutes for the walk—you are west of Eighth Avenue—this is a good pre-theater place, but it is also a good place to linger in pleasant company.

Cocktails, wines and beer.

The menu is à la carte, with midday prices from $3 to $5.25; in the evening from $4.25 to $6.75.

Open 7 days a week, except summer. Open Monday through Saturday from noon until 11:00 p.m.; Sunday until 11:30 p.m.

Closed on Saturday from Memorial to Labor Day. Also closed for lunch only on all major holidays.

Reservations recommended.

AE

★ CAFE DU CENTRE

152 Columbus Avenue (between 66th & 67th Streets)
799-2254
    The impression is that this very small restaurant tucked away in the cluster of others serving the Lincoln Center area is the project of enthusiastic and talented young amateurs. You may find some unevenness as the typical result but it is a pretty spot and the efforts at imaginative cooking—in a general way, French—are more often successful than not. When this kind of restaurant with its determination to please is compared with the deteriorated professionalism of, for instance, Le Poulailler, a big, well-established confrère in the area, you are ready to forgive the little fellow any occasional lapses.

Cocktails, wines and beer.

There is a daily luncheon special at $3.25. A la carte items at lunch cost from about $2.25 to $3.95. The à la carte menu at dinner is from about $5.25 to $9.00; complete dinner $1.50 more. After-theatre appetizers available from $1.50 up.

Open 7 days a week from noon until 11:30 p.m. Call for brunch hours.

Reservations accepted.

Dinner music.

No credit cards.

★★ CAFE EUROPA & LE BRIOCHE

347 East 54th Street (near First Avenue)   755-0160
    Much effort has been made to give Café Europa an original personality, and on the whole it is successful. The decoration, including some genuinely old paintings, is ingenious (and faintly precious), and the piped music runs to composers like Vivaldi. The menu is also original in its specialty of large brioches

hollowed out and filled with curried beef, chicken with ham and peppers, shrimps in sour cream, veal Marengo, or crab gumbo. There is also a menu of such familiar items as orange duck, lamb chops, chicken Kiev, and beef Stroganoff or Wellington. With good food at moderate prices, the tables are well filled. Better reserve.

Cocktails, wines and beer.

At lunch, à la carte dishes cost from about $2.75 to $4.75. A la carte dishes at dinner are from $4.25; table d'hôte dinners cost from $8.00 to $11.00.

Open Monday through Saturday from noon to 11:30 p.m.

Closed Sunday, all major holidays and from December 23rd to January 7th.

Reservations recommended. After-theatre reservations accepted.

AE   BA   CB   DC   MC

★★★ CAFE NICHOLSON
323 East 58th Street   355-6769

The closest thing New York offers to the rabbit's hole leading to Alice's Wonderland is the narrow hallway entered through an inconspicuous doorway leading to the Café Nicholson's elaborately fanciful rooms. The place offered a field day to its decorator, and the excellent food is served with appropriate flourishes. With its air of seclusion from the rest of the world, this is a fine place to entertain guests who want elegance without excitement.

Cocktails, wines and beer.

Open for dinner only with prix fixe dishes from about $17.50 to $19.50 including wine. A la carte menu in new Café Lounge opened in September 1975; call for prices.

Open from Monday through Saturday from 7:00 to 9:30 p.m. From 5:00 p.m. until 11:30 p.m. in new Café Lounge.

Closed Sunday, all major holidays and the last 2 weeks in August and the first 2 weeks in September.

Reservations accepted.

There are two private dining rooms for banquets and parties. One seats up to 14, the other up to 30 guests.

AE   CB   DC

★★ CAPTAIN'S TABLE, THE

410 Avenue of the Americas (near 8th Street)   473-0670

The simpler your choice here, the better it is likely to be. For that matter, the restaurant doesn't try any very fancy specialties. The great virtue is the one that should be paramount in any fish restaurant—the freshness of the ingredients. There's nothing stylish in either the service or the decor. But it's good fish.

Cocktails, wines and beer.

At lunch, entrées cost from about $2.50 to $3.50; at dinner, dishes are from $4.50 to $8.50. Both served with potato, vegetable of the day and salad.

Open 7 days a week. Open from noon to 11:00 p.m. Monday through Thursday; Friday and Saturday from noon till midnight, Sunday 2:00 p.m. until 10:00 p.m.

Closed Christmas.

Reservations accepted for lunch.

AE   CB   MC

★★ CARROUSEL

1307 Third Avenue (at 79th Street)   744-4978

Brand new as we go to press, Carrousel looks as if it is here to stay. Listing only six hors d'oeuvre and nine entrées, the dinner menu doesn't carry you very far afield, but everything we tried on two occasions impressed us as first rate with the exception of the filet of bass en croûte, which, probably because it sounds most unusual, seems to be the most popular entrée. We can vouch for just about anything else on the menu, with a special pat on the back for the feuilleté au Roquefort and mushrooms Catalane.

The front room is a very attractive little bistro with etched glass partitions dividing it from the bar. Try to get a table there.

Cocktails, wines and beer.

All dishes are à la carte, with main courses at midday from about $3.50 to $6.50; in the evening, from about $6.50 to $9.50.

Open Monday through Saturday from noon till 10:30 p.m. Closed Sunday.

Reservations accepted for lunch, recommended for dinner.
AE   DC   MC

★★★ CASA BRASIL
406 East 85th Street   288-5284

This is definitely one not to miss, whether you go on a Wednesday, when the menu is Brazilian, or one of the other nights of the week, when it is continental. In any case, reservations are imperative. The Casa Brasil is a tiny place, beautifully appointed, intimately lit, maybe a bit crowded but comfortable all the same. Ordinarily you are offered your choice of three entrées, which vary from time to time but can be depended on to be excellent, and the rest of the meal comes along with it. On Wednesdays it's the national dish of Brazil, feijoada, a mixture of black beans, roast pork, rice, sausages, tongue, orange sections, and some mandioca flour (made from a South American tuber). No need to be afraid of it.

There is no liquor but customers may bring their own wine.

Open for dinner only. There is a prix fixe at $14.00.

There are two sittings at 7:00 p.m. and at 9:30 p.m. Monday through Saturday.

Closed Sunday, all major holidays and the last 2 weeks in July and the first week in August.

Reservations required.

No credit cards.   PC

★★★ CASEY'S

142 West 10th Street   255-5382

Given the name and the address, you'd expect a pub-type restaurant or maybe a chophouse. What you find is a very good and rather expensive French restaurant differing from some of the best uptown primarily in a more informal décor and the vastness of the portions. Counting the shells after an opener of moules vinaigrette, which we had been foresighted enough to share between two, we found four dozen. It was a tribute to the sole bonne femme and veal scaloppine in cream sauce—four of these with a veritable mountain of noodles—that we consumed about half of each order. The question is, when food is good enough for gourmets, why do they offer it as if to gluttons?

Service at Casey's is excellent.

Cocktails, wines and beer.

All dishes are à la carte, with main courses at midday from about $3.25 to $6.25; in the evening, from about $8.25 to $15.00. Brunch costs from $1.50 to $7.50.

Open 7 days a week from noon to midnight. Saturday and Sunday brunch from noon to 3:30 p.m.

Closed major holidays.

Reservations accepted for lunch, recommended for dinner.
AE   DC   MC

★ **CASTILIAN ROOM**
303 East 56th Street   688-6435
    This smallish room has the artificially rough-
ened plaster walls and heavy darkened wooden divi-
sions and pseudo-beams that seem to be de rigueur for
Spanish restaurants in New York, although we can't
remember having run into any similar ones in Spain.
The food is also pretty standard, from gazpacho to
paella to flan, varying from excellent to satisfactory.
It is a nice, quiet place, dimly lit but not so dark that
you can't see your plate, as in some restaurants. Service is courteous, and the general end result quite pleas-
urable.

Cocktails, wines and beer.
The à la carte menu is priced from about $4.00 to $7.00
at lunch. At dinner, à la carte dishes cost from about $5.50
to $8.75.
Open 7 days a week from noon until midnight.
Reservations accepted.
AE   CB

★★★ **CHALET SUISSE**
6 East 48th Street   355-0855
    This isn't exactly the least expensive restaurant
in New York but it is a consistently good one and
you're not likely to feel cheated. On different visits we
have racked up as much as $50 for two people, and as
little as $25, at dinner. Lunch of course is a little
less.
    The food is hearty but not overpowering, and at-
tractively served by pleasant, efficient waitresses.
Among the dishes we have liked a lot, the favorite
appetizer is délice d'Emmenthal, crescents of this
cheese in a light batter, deep-fried and served piping

hot, looking for all the world like small plantains and yielding a delicious goo when you puncture the crust. The three of these were plenty in a divided order for two of us. Among the entrées, our favorite was perhaps Rock Cornish game hen prepared "Poire William." These birds are frequently miserable little creatures by the time they reach the table but the ones we've had at Chalet Suisse have been plump and juicy with a sauce of the pear liqueur and a stuffing of the fruit itself.

There are also excellent fondues here. You're pretty safe, as a matter of fact, in whatever you order. If you have enough room left for a dessert, anything with Swiss chocolate is a must.

Cocktails, wines and beer.

Lunch is à la carte and costs from about $5.75 to $13.50. A la carte entrées at dinner are $6.00 to $13.50; table d'hôte dinner is $12.00.

Open Monday through Friday from 11:45 to 9:30 p.m.

Closed Saturday, Sunday, all major holidays and the month of August.

Reservations required at lunch, recommended at dinner. AE CB DC MC

★★★ CHARLEY O'S BAR AND GRILL

Rockefeller Center, 33 West 48th Street   582-7141

If faked Irish saloon atmosphere is your dish, this is the place for you—begorra. The style is free and easy at the partially self-service sandwich bar, a bit quieter in the main dining room, with pigs' knuckles, ham and cabbage, braised brisket, and roast ribs of beef setting the gastronomic pace. Charley O's late suppers and Sunday brunches are popular with people who keep hours like that.

Cocktails, wines and beer.

All dishes are à la carte, with main courses at midday from about $4.75 to $8.50; in the evening, from about $5.25 to $10.95.

Open Monday through Saturday (see below) from 11:30 to 11:00 p.m.

Closed Sunday and Christmas, New Year's Day, Washington's Birthday, Memorial Day, July 4th and Labor Day. Closed Saturdays between Memorial Day and Veterans Day.

Reservations accepted at dinner.

Sandwich counter open from 11:30 a.m. till 8:30 p.m.

AE   BA   CB   DC   MC

★★ CHARLIE & KELLY

259 West 4th Street (at Perry Street)   675-5059

This restaurant is a charmer, full of hanging and potted plants, seating about 40 people at most, and giving you just about as good value for your money as any restaurant in town.

It is a very personal kind of kitchen; every dish is given a special fillip. For instance, broiled breast of chicken with herbs, not unusual, with lime, which is, served with rice strongly flavored with fennel. Also, fish topped with a purée of horseradish and beets. A plain, straightforward flounder in black butter and white wine is also excellent.

Charlie & Kelly, who offer dinner only, have daily specials and a "fish du jour." They are also proud of their soups, and their desserts are luscious. When we go there we try for one of the tables by the window where we can watch the passers-by on this quiet corner in Greenwich Village.

Cocktails, wines and beer.

Open for dinner only, with dinner entrées from about $5.75 to $8.95 which includes rice, salad and vegetable. Brunch prices range from $2.75 to $3.50.

Open daily from 6:00 p.m. until midnight. Weekend brunch from noon until 4:00 p.m. All cocktails from 4:30 until 7:00 p.m. $1.25 and at brunch. Weekend brunch from noon until 4:00 p.m.

Open 7 days a week. Closed Christmas.

Brunch and weekend reservations recommended.

No credit cards. Credit cards in future; call.   PC

★★ CHATEAU RICHELIEU
48 East 52nd Street   PL 1-6565

Here's a beautifully appointed room, an elegant ambiance, waiters and captains who are suave, courteous, and efficient, a menu it would take you a week to study, and very good food indeed, with emphasis on French regional dishes. This is really an excellent restaurant, and "excellent" is supposed to mean three stars. We are not sure why Chateau Richelieu hasn't had a more enthusiastic reception by restaurant reviewers, but hold back from a third star only because we try to average in the price, and found that what with this and that (including an indulgent $3.75 for oysters Rockefeller as an opener) and well-deserved tips for both waiter and captain, and a bottle of wine in the lower brackets of the list, The tab built up to $66 for a dinner for two, which is a little high.

But we say by all means make the acquaintance of Chateau Richelieu if you don't worry too much about the old wallet. It has a real air about it. We enjoyed sitting there, as well as eating there.

Cocktails, wines and beer.

All dishes are à la carte, with main courses at midday from about $5.50, in the evening, prices begin at $6.50.

*Open from Monday through Saturday from noon until
10:30 p.m. (10:30 is latest to order dinner).*

*Closed Sundays and Christmas, New Year's Day,
Memorial Day, July 4th and the last two weeks in August,
reopening after Labor Day.*

Reservations accepted.

Jackets required for men.

All major credit cards.

★★ CHEZ NAPOLEON

365 West 50th Street   CO 5-6980

A block or two can make all the difference in
New York, and Chez Napoleon is just far enough
away from the center of things to have the air of a
hideaway. It is a small restaurant that seems smaller
for being divided into two rooms, and a good word for
it is "charming."

First off, let's recommend that you try the rabbit in
white wine sauce. You don't like rabbit? Either you
just don't like the idea or you're thinking of civet de
lapin, dark and strong in a sauce made with the blood.
The lapin (if you like the word better than rabbit)
Chez Napoleon is delicate, something like the second
joint of chicken, and the sauce is delectable. Be sure
to sop some bread in it.

This is a family-operated restaurant and the service
is both informal and excellent. They feature striped
bass and it is always fresh and well prepared. "Fresh"
is indeed a general virtue of the food here.

The atmosphere is homey, with a faintly shabby
décor contributing to the effect. It is the kind of small
restaurant that has fans of many years' standing, and
it's easy to understand why.

Cocktails, wines and beer.

A la carte dishes at lunch cost from about $3 to $5; table

*d'hôte from about $4.00 to $6.50. The à la carte menu at
dinner is from $4.50 to $7.00.*

*Open Monday through Saturday from noon until
10:00 p.m.*

Reservations recommended.

AE   BA

★   **CHEZ RAYMOND**

240 West 56th Street   245-3656 and 755-1795

Watch yourself carefully and you can get a full
stomach of fairly good French food (appetizer, soup,
salad, entrée, and dessert) for a reasonable price here,
served in a reasonable facsimile of a good French restaurant. The daily specials are likely to be the best
prepared; they come from the kitchen hot, fresh, and
tasty, as opposed to some of the other dishes on the
ambitious menu, which don't always come off too
well.

Cocktails, wines and beer.

*Complete lunch runs from $6.10 to $8.75; à la carte is less
$1.00. Table d'hôte at dinner is from $9.50 to $12.50. Complete
dinner (chef's special) for two: $26.00. A la carte menu only
on Saturday.*

*Open Monday through Thursday from noon until 10:30;
Friday until 11:00 p.m.; Saturday until midnight.*

*Closed Sunday, New Year's Day, July 4th, Thanksgiving
and Christmas. Also closed from August 23rd to September 8th.*

Reservations recommended.

AE   BA   DC

★★   **CHEZ VOUS**

78 Carmine Street (at Seventh Avenue South)   CH 2-2676

In spite of its name, Chez Vous is vehemently
Italian. Although it advertises North Italian cooking,
we have found our samplings on the more strongly

82

flavored side—and very good, too. Chez Vous has an army of fans who keep it packed most of the time, but for newcomers the welcome is genuinely warm and the service friendly. We have a friend who admired her cocktail glass at the bar and was presented with half a dozen to take home, but this is not a guaranteed policy of the place.

Cocktails, wines and beer.

All dishes are à la carte, with main courses at midday starting at $3.75 and up; in the evening, from about $3.25 to $8.50 (the $8.50 representing a 1¼ lb. prime beef steak, no bone, no fat).

Open Monday through Saturday from 11:30 a.m. to 11:00 p.m.

Closed Sunday and major holidays.

Reservations recommended.

BA   DC   MC

★★★★ CHRIST CELLA

160 East 46th Street   OX 7-2479

This steak house, just about the best and busiest within our experience, has a quiet international reputation. It's a place of no frills, no fancy specialties, and no nonsense, yet in its direct, professional way it has as much style as any restaurant in town. Take the waiters out of their uniforms of black trousers, white shirt, long white apron, and dark red tie and put them in cap and gown, and they could be the stars of any academic procession.

Christ Cella is a big restaurant, but the division into small rooms gives the opposite impression. It can get a little noisy.

There's no printed menu. You order from a captain who takes it for granted that you know what the restaurant offers—steaks, fish, seafood, and chicken, with baked, french fried, or hashed brown potatoes, salads, and a limited selection of vegetables.

Christ Cella's is usually crowded, but our experience has been that they are very good about honoring reservations.

Cocktails, wines and beer.

The à la carte menu for lunch is from $7.50 to $12.50; dinner is from $8.50 to $12.50 (for steaks).

Open Monday through Saturday (except summer dinner, see below) from 11:30 until the last seating at 10:30 p.m.

Closed Sunday and July and August Saturday dinner. Also closed Thanksgiving, Christmas, New Year's Day, Memorial Day and July 4th.

Reservations recommended.

AE   BA   CB   DC   MC

★★ COACH HOUSE, THE

110 Waverly Place   777-0303

Many a person, including some serious gourmets, say flatly that The Coach House is the best restaurant in New York. That hasn't been our experience. Service has been indifferent at times, and the food far from uniformly excellent. But for the restaurant-goer who complains that good American food is hard to find, with all those French and Italian and Chinese restaurants getting so much attention, the Coach House offers such specialties as black bean soup, steaks, charcoal-broiled lamb chops, and pecan pie.

Cocktails, wines and beer.

At lunch, à la carte dishes cost from about $4.50 to $8.00; table d'hôte from $7.50 to $10.50. A la carte entrées at dinner are from $7.00 to $13.00; table d'hôte dinners from $14.50 to $18.75.

84

Open Tuesdays through Sundays from noon until 10:00 p.m.

Closed Mondays, Christmas, New Year's Day, 4th of July, Labor Day, Thanksgiving and the month of August.

Reservations recommended at lunch, required at dinner.
AE CB DC MC

★★★ CORIANDER

314 East 72nd Street   794-2700

Let's say immediately that Coriander is a very noisy restaurant, largely because people are enjoying themselves so much. The convivial air in small quarters is the result of a clientele that comes back and back to the place as a kind of semi-club. But you're perfectly welcome.

Coriander has one of the most varied menus in town, the chef, Joel Levy, having been a globe-trotter with an interest in cooking. He cheffed in Bangkok for a period and offers a number of Thai dishes. Among these the shrimp lemon soup—a thin peppery broth strongly flavored with lemon in which you find a couple of perfect shrimp, some raw mushrooms, bits of other vegetables, and fresh herbs complete with stems —is not to be missed if it is available the evening of your visit.

The à la carte menu offers the ultimate simplicity of a hamburger if that's your mood. We prefer such specialties as chicken Gaiyand, half a broiled chicken served with hot and sweet sauce with a strong Indonesian cast, calamari alla marina, deep-batter-fried fresh squid, and tile fish when the restaurant can find it. The tile, itself a gourmet, feeds on lobsters at depths of about 300 feet and gets to market infrequently, but when it does, Coriander combines it with a topping including gumbo file (a powdered seasoning) to provide a concentrated accent for the very dry, white, delicately flavored fish in thick, crumbling slabs.

Finally, whatever your entrée, moo saté is an ideal opener. These strips of pork on wooden skewers served with peanut curry sauce are perfect.

Cocktails, wines and beer.

Open for dinner only. The à la carte menu is priced from about $4.25 to $10.95.

Open daily from 6:00 p.m. thru midnight.

Telephone inquiry suggested for vacation and holiday closings.

Reservations recommended.

AE DC

★ CRAWDADDY

45 East 45th Street   889-8331

If Crawdaddy's kitchen ever manages to live up to its décor, it will be one of the best restaurants in New York. As it is, it is one of the most attractive, whether you're in the bar-lounge, the oyster bar, or the dining room. Traditional New Orleans restaurant style is followed with mirrors, thickly applied white enamel on the woodwork, and white tile floor. If you know Galatoire's, in New Orleans, you'll get homesick. The menu, rather limited, offers approximations of New Orleans specialties, of which oysters Rockefeller were acceptable when we tried them, and shrimp rémoulade not.

Cocktails, wines and beer.

The à la carte menu at lunch is priced from $3.50 and up; at dinner from $5.25 and up.

Open from Monday through Friday from 11:45 until the last seating at 9:15 p.m.

Closed Saturday, Sunday and all major holidays.
Reservations accepted for dinner.
Sandwich counter available.
All major credit cards.

★★ CZECHOSLOVAK PRAHA
1358 First Avenue (at 73rd Street)   *988-3505*

Goose, dumplings, sauerkraut, rabbit in cream sauce, goulash, stuffed cabbage—this menu shouldn't even be read unless you have a hearty appetite. Czechoslovak Praha, partially Americanized, also lists southern fried chicken and western omelet, but goes in heavily for reminders of the homeland, including strolling musicians. It is a place for what you might call a very full evening rather than a quiet, relaxed one. The bar is also lively.

Cocktails, wines and beer.
At lunch, à la carte dishes cost from about $2.00 to $7.50.
Table d'hôte dinners are from $5.25 to $8.95.
Open 7 days a week from noon until 11:00 p.m.
Reservations accepted.
AE

★★★ DARDANELLES ARMENIAN RESTAURANT
86 University Place   CH 2-8990

Dardanelles is a bright, cheerful restaurant with an unpretentious air of informal elegance set by a big bouquet of flowers just as you enter. The service is exemplary, and if you aren't sure you know your way around in the Armenian food field, your waiter will enjoy helping you out. If you do know it, you will recognize the excellence of such standard dishes as shish kebab, prepared here in ways that give them a special zest. The rice (always a test of a Near Eastern kitchen, like pasta in an Italian one) is just right —herbed, flavorsome, not too soft, each grain separate.

For an opening sampler, the "Dardanelles Special," a medley of appetizers, is good. We also enjoyed targhana as an overture—yogurt soup prepared with chopped onions and mint leaves.

Although it can't be guaranteed as a regular feature, Dardanelles from time to time has excellent music at dinner performed on the oud by a young man who improvises on traditional dances and folk songs.

Wines and beer.

The à la carte luncheon items cost from about $3.45 to $3.65. A la carte entrées at dinner start from $5.50; table d'hôte dinners are from $8.00 and up. There is a weekday dinner special for $5.95 which includes salad and coffee.

Open daily (except summer, see below) from noon. Monday through Thursday from noon until 10:00 p.m.; Friday and Saturday until 11:00 p.m.; Sundays from 4:00 to 9:00 p.m.

Closed Sunday for lunch and all day Sunday July and August. Also closed all major holidays.

Reservations accepted.

Live ethnic music on Saturday.

AE   CB   DC   MC

★★ DeCUIR'S

1244 Madison Avenue (between 89th and 90th Streets)
289-7470

DeCuir's specializes in New Orleans creole dishes, and can serve a thumping three-star meal when not pressed. But it can go to pieces so badly, not honoring reservations, letting you wait for an hour at your table if you get one, and losing its head generally, that a cautious two stars are plenty. The trouble—and the virtue—of the restaurant is that it is essentially an amateur project, with "amateur" meaning a talented chef in the kitchen and some student-type waiters in the dining room.

Otherwise—well, the seafood gumbo is the very essence of that hybrid between a thick soup and a wet hash; the duck à l'orange is superlative; pompano amandine, salmon steak meunière, and filet mignon en croute have delighted us. The room is attractive, the intentions are noble, and the performance—let's hope you don't hit a busy night.

Cocktails, wines and beer.

Table d'hôte luncheons are priced from about $3.95 to $5.50; table d'hôte dinners from $8.95 to $10.50.

Open from Monday through Saturday from 11:30 until 11:00 p.m.

Closed Sunday. Phone for holiday and vacation closings.

Reservations accepted.

AE   BA   DC

★ DELFINO'S

68 Fifth Avenue (between 12th and 13th Streets)   OR *5-7379*

Delfino's is particularly recommended for lunch, when a cheerful congregation enjoys well-prepared standard dishes such as scaloppine piccata or Marsala or a house specialty not on the menu— brodetto, a fish soup that varies depending on which fish and other seafood is available in the market. Dinner is very quiet, and this restaurant, with a lively kind of decoration, somehow needs a lively bunch of diners. There is dancing on Friday and Saturday nights, which no doubt changes things, but we have never stayed for it.

Cocktails, wines and beer.

Table d'hôte luncheons are from $4.95 to $8.95; complete dinners are priced from about $6.50 to $9.50.
Open Monday through Saturday from noon until 1:00 a.m.
Closed Sunday.
Reservations accepted at lunch.
AE BA DC MC

★★ DELSOMMA
266 West 47th Street   PL *7-9079*
   Some New Yorkers might question the legitimacy of a second star for Delsomma and in fact we gave it only one in a report about a year ago. But it earns a second on longevity and continued dependability. Delsomma's has been around for 17 years to my own knowledge without changing very much, and it also has the capacity to make you feel at home in 17 minutes, or less. The general tone is something like that of the old-time neighborhood Italian restaurant, although this is much larger. It combines a casual air with efficient management.
   It's a good idea to ask for your pasta al dente or you might get it a little overcooked. Also, be prepared for generous quantities of olive oil in many dishes. The cooking isn't subtle, but Delsomma's can boast that it has made repeaters out of many New Yorkers—including this reporter—over many years.
Cocktails, wines and beer.
The prix fixe lunch is $3.90. Dinners are à la carte and start at $3.80.
Open Monday through Saturday from noon until midnight.
Closed Sunday and Christmas.
Reservations recommended.
AE BA CB DC

90

★ DEWEY WONG

206 East 58th Street 758-6881

Dewey Wong's, an amiable place, is a holdover from the type of Chinese restaurant that seemed both elegant and exotic to New Yorkers when there were very few outside Chinatown except for chop suey joints. People who are not attracted by the authenticity and sophistication of the new crop of Chinese restaurants, will find Dewey Wong's still tops.

Cocktails, wines and beer.

Special lunch is from $3.25 to $6.80, with the à la carte menu also available. The à la carte dinner is from $3.10 to $10.25.

Open 7 days a week. Open Monday through Saturday from noon until midnight; open Sunday from 3:00 p.m. until midnight.

Closed July 4th and Thanksgiving. Call for holiday closing.

Reservations accepted.

AE   DC   MC

★ DI ANNI'S

1122 First Avenue (at 62nd Street) 838-2230

At the moment of writing, this brand new restaurant with interesting ideas is still trying to get its bearings, but it looks like good things ahead. A section of the menu is devoted to "Cuisine Historique," or "fine dishes served at the courts of Kings, Queens and Nobles on festive occasions long ago." The food isn't quite all that special as yet, but the kitchen is valiant and its product is superior to the general run elsewhere at the prices, which, in Di Anni's word, are "compassionate." The atmosphere is pleasant.

Cocktails, wine and beer.

Open for dinner only (lunch is planned for future). A la carte appetizers are from $1.75 to $2.75; entrées begin at $4.25 and include salad, vegetable and potato.

Open 7 nights a week from 6:00 p.m. until 1:00 a.m.

Closed Thanksgiving, Christmas and New Year's Day.

Reservations not necessary.

Special dishes for 2 persons or more may be ordered 24 hours in advance.

AE   BA   DC   MC

★★ DIOGENES

937 Eighth Avenue (between 55th and 56th Streets)
586-0470

Here's a very attractive Greek restaurant, eager to please, that combines some excellent Greek specialties with a rather wide choice of Continental and American dishes if you're not all that keen on Greek food. If you like it, you will enjoy their specialty, exohico drosias, described as "a delightful lamb dish from the Athenian countryside." It's a mixture of lamb, vegetables, and herbs in a casing of the many-leaved tissue-thin pastry called phyllo, and delightful is the right word for it when it's properly prepared.

We also remember with pleasure the garides falirou, shrimp baked with tomato, onion, and feta cheese. Among the non-Greek dishes, we found a simple broiled striped bass excellent.

Service here is super-attentive without being over-solicitous. And a very pleasant aspect of the place is that the tables are never too close together. Several are tucked off in pleasant corners where you can feel private even while being part of the dining room. The semi-partitions of wood slats are supposed to suggest the inside of Diogenes's barrel.

Cocktails, wines and beer.

All dishes are à la carte, with main courses at midday from about $3.50 to $5.50; in the evening, from about $5.50 to $10.00. A brunch menu is being planned but there is an after-theatre special, Diogenes Mezedakia, at $5.95.

Open from Monday through Saturday from noon until midnight.

Reservations are recommended.

AE   DC   MC

★ **DORRIAN'S RED HAND**
1616 Second Avenue (at 84th Street)   650-1016

This is essentially a French bistro in spite of pastas, shish kebabs, and gazpacho on the international menu. Preparation, which is acceptable to excellent, tends to be better than the raw materials in some cases. Steaks, for instance, come with excellent sauces but haven't always been the greatest pieces of beef in the world to begin with. By which we don't mean that anything is wrong in the kitchen as far as your health is concerned; rather, this helps explain the moderate prices at Dorrian's. The décor, tending toward turn-of-the-century pub style, is not too bad, and the wine list includes some good numbers at modest prices.

Cocktails, wines and beer.

All dishes are à la carte, with main courses at midday from about $2.80 to $3.50; in the evening from about $5.25 to $10.25.

Open daily from 11:00 until 2:00 a.m. There is a Sunday brunch from 10:30 a.m. until 4:30 p.m.

Open 7 days a week.

Closed Easter and Christmas.

Reservations accepted.
AE   DC   MC

★   **EL MIRADOR**
899 First Avenue (between 50th and 51st Streets)   PL 5-5536
     According to our dictionary "mirador" means
a high balcony in Spain looking out over a vista, or
a penthouse in Mexico City with a view. The best
view El Mirador offers is a sharply curtailed street-
level segment of First Avenue traffic, but it does better
in the food division.

One of the few Mexican restaurants that even tries
to make a mole verde, El Mirador manages a reasonable facsimile, for which we are grateful. The rest of
the menu is typically limited, but preparation is very
good, and prices are reasonable.
     Wines and beer.
     The à la carte luncheon is from $3 to $3.50, which includes
rice, beans and salad. A la carte entrées at dinner cost $4.50
to $7.00.
     Open 7 days a week from noon until 11:00 p.m.
     Reservations recommended.
     No credit cards.

★★★   **EL PARADOR**
325 East 34th Street   679-6812
     El Parador is as close as New York comes to
having an elegant Mexican restaurant. It still lacks a
great Mexican chef, and the food is in fact as Spanish
as it is Mexican, but the appurtenances of civilized
dining are at least recognized as applicable to Mexican
cuisine, as opposed to the usual idea that Mexico is
entirely made up of rough and ready rancheros and
huarached peons. Once you get past the proprietor's

greeting, which is too affectionate, the service is properly amiable.

Cocktails, wines and beer.

Open for dinner only, with à la carte dishes from about $5.50 to $6.75.

Open Monday through Saturday from 5:00 p.m. to 11:00 p.m.

Closed Sunday, major holidays and the first 3 weeks in July.

No reservations accepted.

No credit cards.

★ EL SOMBRERO

239 East 86th Street   289-9547

Pending the advent of a classical Mexican restaurant in New York, apparently an unlikely eventuality, you can do a lot worse than mark time at El Sombrero. It does well, within the standard range from tamales to the reasonable facsimile of mole poblano that we gringos have to settle for, and we even found one relatively adventurous dish, chicken in green sauce, on the menu. The large chunks of white meat in a thin bath of herbs, mildly peppered, were delectable. If you order this, however, better get side orders of salad and either rice or refried beans to balance things out.

Forget the guacamole. It's slush made, for sure, in a blender.

The décor is based on the principle that any spot left uncovered is embarrassing, with the result that the walls are hung with a clutter of serapes, guitars, sequined sombreros, big paper flowers, feather pictures, naïve oil paintings, piñatas, and whatever other bits of picturesque Mexicana you can think of. El

Sombrero is usually pretty well filled, which isn't surprising, since it's a jolly place and not all that expensive.

Cocktails, wines and beer.

Open for dinner only with à la carte dishes from about $4.50 to $9.00.

Open 7 days a week from 3:00 p.m. until 3:00 a.m.

Reservations recommended.

All major credit cards.

★★ EXPERIENCE

408 East 64th Street   355-8926

The name suggests that maybe you are going to be subjected to some kind of novelty treatment, but the restaurant's virtue is its dedication to the most conventional standards of enjoyable dining, beginning with the room's muted red walls, the snowy tablecloths, and the sparkling glasses. Tables are nicely spaced, service is attentive, and we were happy with such dishes as orange duck, paillard of beef, and veal cordon bleu.

Cocktails, wines and beer.

Open for dinner only with à la carte entrées costing from $5.95 and up. Rack of lamb for two is $19.95.

Open Monday through Saturday from 6:00 until 11:00 p.m.

Closed all legal holidays. Call for vacation closings.

Reservations recommended.

AE

★★ FILOXENIA

475 Park Avenue (at 57th Street)   838-1717

Filoxenia—the name means "Hospitality"—is the most elegantly decorated Greek restaurant in New York, sleek but warm, and on the basis of one of our visits—the first—we'd have been willing to say it had the best Greek food. The moussaka, a dish that has a range from rough country fare to haute cuisine, was delicate, fragrant, and exquisitely flavored; a house specialty, veal chop pescador (sautéed, with shrimp and mousseline sauce) was delightful, and a striped bass with fresh tomatoes, feta cheese, and herbs, was a triumph. The service was equal to the food.

On a second visit neither food nor service was anything to get excited about, and on a third both were inferior. We learned later that our third visit was made on the regular chef's day off, but that did not excuse the lackadaisical service. The restaurant may have straightened all that out by now, but the best we can do in a report is to say that Filoxenia is an extremely attractive restaurant where you may get something close to four-star food and service or where you may think our two stars are generous. Good luck. It's definitely worth a try.

Cocktails, wines and beer.

All dishes are à la carte, with main courses at midday from about $4.74 to $7.50; in the evening, from about $5.75 to $8.50. Brunch is from the à la carte menu but is not available during the summer.

Open 7 days a week, except for summer, from noon until 12:30 a.m. Closed Sunday during summer.

Reservations recommended.

AE BA DC MC

★★ FONDA LA PALOMA
256 East 49th Street (between 2nd and 3rd Avenues)
421-5495

    This Mexican restaurant has a more extensive menu than most, including a reasonable mole verde.

We are kept away by a feature that, on the contrary, may attract you—strolling mariachis whose music would be good to listen to out on the plaza but is deafening at your table. People seem to like it, however, since it has been a feature of Fonda la Paloma for years.

Cocktails, wines and beer.

At lunch, à la carte dishes cost from about $4.50 to $5.75 with coffee and dessert included. A la carte dishes at dinner are from $5.75 to $7.50.

Open 7 days a week from noon until midnight.

Closed all major holidays.

Reservations accepted.

Mariachi music nightly.

All major credit cards.

★★ FONDA LOS MILAGROS

70 East 55th Street   752-6640

It seems odd that New York, with its wide variety of national cuisines, has restaurants that rival the best in their native lands with the exception of Mexico. The reason is partly that some of the ingredients are unavailable—special types of fresh chiles and certain herbs. But that's only part of it. Many can be found at Mexican and Puerto Rican markets by anyone interested enough in hunting them out. Where the Mexican restaurants fail is in not taking advantage of the variety and subtlety of Mexican dishes, probably because they take elaborate preparation. So we get a standard limited sampling of chili, tamales, enchiladas, tacos, and at best an approximation of mole poblano.

Fonda los Milagros makes a more serious effort than most North American Mexican restaurants to explore

98

the genuine article, even being one of the few places in town that tries a mole verde. It's fair. They have some zesty appetizers, and the guacamole, always a test, passes with honors. "Fonda los Milagros" means "Inn of the Miracles" and these don't materialize, but still, a second star is merited for effort in the right direction.

Cocktails, wines and beer.

The dishes at lunch are from about $3.25 to $6.00, which includes rice, beans, dessert and coffee. The à la carte menu at dinner is from $4.25 to $7.00.

Open Monday through Saturday from 11:30 a.m. until midnight.

Closed Sunday and all major holidays.

Reservations recommended.

All major credit cards.

★ **FOUR SEASONS, THE**
99 East 52nd Street   PL4-9494

Whatever became of that beautiful restaurant in the Seagram Building—remember? The one with a pool in the middle of the room and live trees they changed with the seasons.

The Four Seasons, yes. A beautiful restaurant with food to match. Then it had its ups and downs and changes of management. Lately, we heard, it was away up again, and by the evidence of a dinner party given there by an acquaintance who pre-arranged a special menu, the kitchen can turn out food that's hard to beat. But our last check-up on the Four Seasons, just before going to press with this guide, was disastrous. The elegance is a bit tarnished, plain old all-purpose all-season rubber plants now stand by the poolside, and there aren't even any flowers on the tables, which, at the prices, the restaurant could certainly afford. We had, however, excellent food. But we had, as well, deplorable service, devoid of both efficiency and style. It was an unsatisfactory and expensive evening.

A colleague reports more favorably on the café, open for lunch near the popular bar.

Cocktails, wines and beer.

All dishes are à la carte, with main courses at midday from about $6.25 and up; in the evening, from about $8.25. There is a prix fixe pre-theatre special supper at $13.50.

Open Monday through Saturday from noon until 11:00 p.m.

Closed Sunday, Christmas, New Year's Day, Memorial Day, 4th of July and Labor Day.

Reservations required at lunch, recommended at dinner.

All major credit cards.

★★ FRENCH SHACK, THE
65 West 55th Street   CI *6-5126*

The French Shack—which is thoroughly French but in no way a shack—is heartily recommended to anyone who has an unlimited capacity for the ingestion of tremendous portions of food, and also to anyone who likes good French food and doesn't mind leaving about half the portion on the plate to be thrown in the garbage. We do mind, but with that reservation have found this a very good restaurant indeed.

Several of the entrées on the extensive menu are stamped "Recommandé" and you're safe in sticking to them. Among the appetizers, there's a meal-sized seafood pancake maison, very rich and first-rate. The "petit" hors d'oeuvre makes up a mountainous plate of just about everything in the standard hors d'oeuvre list.

If the appetizers haven't stultified your appetite, there's a lamb cassoulet in the style of Toulouse that will complete the job. Roast duck, which comes with wild rice or apples, is also excellent here. For something more bland, we have found poached stuffed trout satisfactory.

Desserts are also interesting, if you can get that far. There are apricot fritters, pears in tequila, and the usual list of favorites such as chocolate mousse and crème caramel.

Cocktails, wines and beer.

Table d'hôte luncheon is from $6.50 to $8.75. Dinners are à la carte, with main courses from about $5.75 to $8.75.

Open 7 days a week. Monday through Thursday and Sunday from noon until 10:00 p.m.; Friday until 10:30 p.m.; Saturday until 11:00 p.m.

Closed Christmas, New Year's Day, July 4th and Labor Day.

Reservations required at lunch, recommended at dinner.

AE   BA   CB   DC   MC

★★   **FRINI**

271 Amsterdam Avenue between 72 and 73rd Streets
TR *4-8950*

Although it calls itself a "Flamenco restaurant," Frini is longer on Mexican and South American dishes than Spanish, and some of these are extraordinary. Strictly on the food, at moderate prices, this is easily a three-star restaurant, but two is safer for a place where your ashtray is dumped into your plate and the other dishes stacked in front of you when the table is cleared. This is the major indication of an atmosphere that is casual to say the least.

Among the specialties, the Venezuelan Hallaca is special indeed—a mixture of chicken, pork, raisins, olives, capers, onions, bacon and sweet red peppers rolled up in the best cornmeal casing you ever tasted. You might watch out also for a Mexican dish, Chile Jalapeño à la Frini. Jalapeño peppers are pure green fire and usually pre-soaked or given other treatment to reduce their intensity before being served except as a fiery accent. In this dish they are stuffed whole and are virtually uncooked. Marvelous if that's your taste; dangerous if not.

Wines and beer.

A la carte dishes at lunch are $2.95, which includes coffee. A la carte dinner is from about $3.95 to $5.95 with coffee. After-theatre special supper is from $3.50 to $5.95.

Open Tuesday through Sunday from 11:30 a.m. until 2:00 a.m. Sunday brunch is from 11:30 until 2:00 p.m.

Reservations recommended.

Paraguayan harp nitely.

AE CB DC MC

★★ GAETANO'S

242 East 58th Street   759-4660

No menu here. The waiter tells you what your choice of entrées is for the night, and the rest follows naturally. It is good food, rather rich. There is a super-picturesque ceiling consisting of demijohns suspended upside down. Also, lots of dim red lights making for a cavelike interior—the Red, rather than the Blue, Grotto. Allow yourself plenty of time for an enjoyable meal.

Cocktails, wines and beer.

Open for dinner only with a prix fixe menu that changes

every Monday at $12.00.

Open from Monday through Saturday from 5:30 to 11:00 p.m.

Closed Sunday and the last 2 weeks in August.

Reservations recommended.

AE   BA   CB   DC

★★★   GAVROCHE

222 East 58th Street   838-0279

Gavroche, very small, is obviously run with loving attention to detail that makes it one of the best restaurants of its size and type in New York. From the china and napery to the wallpaper and the table flowers, everything is a harmonious decorative unit. The same sense of style—along with good cookery —extends to the food. The crudités (raw vegetables) as appetizers come in a basket as artfully arranged as a painting. The quiche, among the other appetizers, is especially good. So is the house salad of greens, walnuts, and Swiss cheese. You're safe enough with any of the entrées.

Cocktails and wines.

At lunch, à la carte dishes cost from about $3.45 to $7.65. A la carte entrées at dinner are from $5.95 to $12.50 with a special 5-course dinner at $9.95.

Open 7 days a week from noon until 1:00 a.m.

Reservations recommended.

There is live entertainment—guitarist or flutist—on Friday, Saturday, Sunday and Monday.

AE   BA   DC   MC

★★ GAYLORD

50 East 58th Street (between Madison and Park Avenues)
759-1710

Gaylord might deserve a third star strictly for atmosphere. The food is sometimes three star, sometimes not. The service often falls down. But the Anglo-Indian atmosphere is something you'd have to go to Gaylord's other restaurants in New Delhi, Bombay, and London to find. Whether some decorator of genius set out to create it or whether it just happened, we can't say, but there it is—strictly pukka, at once exotic and sturdy.

Anyone going to an Indian restaurant probably already has his own ideas as to what he wants to order, but we have to say that the lamb pasanda—tender chunks in a gently flavored sauce that is a wonderful addition to the rice—is a must at Gaylord. In general Gaylord's seasoning is more bland than you will find in India, but this seems to be the rule on this side of the water—which is a shame, for it is the spices, sometimes fiery, sometimes sweet and fragrant, that individualize Indian dishes and make a true Indian meal a series of happy contrasts.

Gaylord is one of the rare New York restaurants that includes service charge (the standard 15 percent) on the check. Better look at yours to see whether this is still the custom; we've known people who didn't notice, and left another 15 percent on the table for the waiter.

Cocktails, wines and beer.

A la carte entrées at lunch are from $6.00 up. The à la carte menu at dinner costs from about $8 to $10 with a prix fixe at $6.95.

Open from Monday through Friday: lunch from 11:30 to

3:00 p.m.; drinks from 3:30 to 5:00 p.m.; dinner from 5:50 to
11:00 p.m. Open Saturday and Sunday from 5:30 until 11:00
p.m.

Closed Saturday and Sunday for lunch and Christmas.
Reservations recommended.
AE   BA   DC

★ **GENGHIZ KHAN'S BICYCLE**
197 Columbus Avenue (corner of 69th Street)   595-2138
We tend to avoid restaurants with cute names,
but a good Turk told us to visit this one for some real
Turkish food after we had enthusiastically reviewed
Bosphorus East—which he said was not Turkish but
Armenian. Well, the food at Genghiz Khan, whatever
its nationality, is good but far from sensational. The
restaurant itself, however, is attractively designed,
with a balcony where backgammon goes on. And—
our main reason for including it—it is fairly close to
Lincoln Center but less likely than those very close
to be crowded before performances, although it can
get jammed later in the evening.

Cocktails, wines and beer.

All dishes are à la carte, with main courses at midday from
about $2.75 to $5.50; in the evening, from about $3.75 to $6.95.
There is a brunch omelet (several choices) with coffee and
Bloody Mary or wine at $3.25.

Open 7 days a week from 11:30 to 1:00 a.m. Brunch is every
day from 11:30 until 4:00 p.m.

Reservations recommended at dinner and after theatre.
There is live dinner music nightly.
AE   MC

★★ GEORGES REY

60 West 55th Street   C15-6764

This is a well-established French restaurant that probably deserves a third star on the basis of the food alone, but we feel that the service becomes a little rushed (which is just as bad as being too slow) when the restaurant is full, and we have also been bothered by bad music badly reproduced over the speakers. The general décor is delightfully French, and the prices are not at all high for superior food. Among the dishes sampled, we particularly liked a poussin aux raisins —young chicken with a light sauce and green grapes.

Cocktails, wines and beer.

All dishes are table d'hôte, with main courses at midday from about $4 to $7; in the evening, from about $7 to $11. After theatre the menu is à la carte and ranges from $1.50 to $6.50.

Open 7 days a week from noon until 11:00 p.m.

Reservations recommended.

AE   BA   MC

★★★ GIAMBELLI

238 Madison Avenue (between 37th and 38th Streets)
MU5-8727

There are two Giambelli restaurants in New York, independently operated. This is the Madison Avenue one, close, incidentally, to the Morgan Library, if you want to combine a visit to one of their exhibitions with an excellent lunch. However, you have to be prepared for a big one, since lunch is prix fixe straight through from appetizer to coffee. Dinner is à la carte. Neither is exactly inexpensive but the food is very good, the restaurant attractive, and the service lively.

At a lunch we found that two of the house specialties, saltimbocca alla Romana (veal scaloppine with
Italian ham and sage) and salsiccia dolce alla Mon-
tanara (sweet pork sausages with fresh peppers and
mushrooms) were excellent choices, combining flair
with the best flavor of standard dishes. These were
preceded by salame Vogherese—half a dozen thin
slices of a small salami highly scented and even more
highly flavored, and escarole and bean soup, which
could hardly have been improved on.

At dinner one night the waiter suggested a pasta
special, small dumplings filled with spinach. First-
rate, divided two ways as a beginner. A plain broiled
sirloin was very good, and a large portion of poached
red snapper fell to pieces at the touch of a fork, as it
should, but wasn't cooked to a mush. If you can take
dessert, the zabaglione here, prepared at your table,
is perfect.

Cocktails, wines and beer.

*At lunch, the table d'hôte dishes cost from $7.00 to $12.50.
Dinner is à la carte, with main courses from $6.50 and up.*

*Open from Monday through Friday (except summer, see
below) from noon until 10:30 p.m.; Saturday until 11:00 p.m.*

*Closed Sunday, major holidays and Saturday during July
and August. Also closed the first two weeks in July.*

Reservations recommended.

AE BA CB DC MC

★★★ GIAN MARINO

221 East 58th Street   PL 2-1696

Mr. Marino's long-established restaurant offers
one of the pleasantest impressions a restaurant can
give you—that you're getting all this attentive service
and good food not because you're going to be paying

for it, but because the staff, from proprietor to bus boys, enjoys doing a good job in a chosen profession. It is an attitude that can double the flavor of a ham on rye at a lunch counter or, when reversed, can vitiate the efforts of the best kitchen.

The menu ranges from North Italian to Sicilian, with a specialty listed from each region, but is predominantly southern. We have been pleased at different times by Venetian calf's liver, very tender, with thin-sliced onions and a delicate sauce; chicken Siciliana, chunks of chicken on the bone in a sauce strongly flavored with garlic; and chicken Sorrentino, a boned half chicken breast alongside a veal scaloppini, each covered by its own large slice of eggplant under a mutual blanket of mozzarella and tomato sauce. This potent combination was offered to us one night when the restaurant was only about half-filled (a blizzard accounted for that rare condition) and is not on the menu, but you could probably get it by asking.

Also, try Gian Marino's linguine with broccoli and zucchini. You can get half orders of any of the 18 pastas.

Cocktails, wines and beer.

All dishes are à la carte, with main courses at midday from about $7.50 to $8.50; in the evening, from about $9.50 to $10.50.

Open 7 days a week from noon until midnight.

Closed Christmas and New Year's Day.

Reservations recommended.

AE BA CB MC

★★ GINO

780 Lexington Avenue (between 60th and 61st Streets)
838-9827

Gino's could be picked as the quintessential New York restaurant if the town's great variety of eating places didn't make that impossible. The clientele is a cross section that includes visiting Italian TV people and writers, who head directly for the place, a good percentage of photographers, some plain family groups, office workers out on a spree, and gastronomes taking a vacation from their more de luxe haunts. With all this, Gino's can get pretty noisy, but at Gino's somehow you not only expect it, but want it.

The food is very Italian and more notable for vigor than for subtlety. There is one specialty, not on the menu, spaghetti segreto, the "secret" part being an excellent sauce that contrasts in its delicacy with the generally robust fare. We're fond of chicken Gino, which is just broiled chicken and garlic with all caution thrown to the winds, and their paillards of either beef or veal.

Gino takes no reservations and there is normally a wait at the bar unless you're early. Although we're frequent visitors we're unknown at Gino's and get no preferential treatment, and we've never been able to catch Gino running a favorite customer in ahead of the waiting line. The service is excellent but necessarily a little on the athletic side.

Cocktails, wines and beer.
The à la carte menu for lunch is priced from about $3.65 to $6.75; dinner entrées are from $5.95 to $8.75.
Open 7 days a week from noon until 10:30 p.m.
Closed Thanksgiving and New Year's Day.

No reservations accepted.
No credit cards.

★ GIORDANO
409 West 39th Street   947-3883-4
    We miss the old Giordano's, a fairly simple, faintly raffish, quite delightful spot where you could relish good, hearty, unpretentious Italian fare. The dishes are now more varied, much richer, and more expensive, with a correspondingly slicked-up décor. It's still a good restaurant. And it has a garden.
Cocktails, beer and wine.
All dishes are à la carte, with main courses at midday from about $4.25 to $9.50; in the evening, from about $5.00 to $10.75.
Open 7 days a week from noon until midnight.
Closed Christmas, New Year's Day and Thanksgiving.
Reservations recommended.
AE   BA   CB   DC   MC

★★★ GIOVANNI
66 East 55th Street   PL 3-1230
    With its diminutive bar at the front of the first floor of an old brownstone, and with two rooms on the second, Giovanni for many years has been one of the most popular intimate restaurants in New York. It is operated with a feeling for style, and gentlemen might as well try to get seated stark naked as without a jacket and tie. Not only Mr. Giovanni—it's a good idea to include the "Mr."—but a number of the waiters as well are senior citizens whose lives are fused with that of the restaurant.
    If the elegance has become ever so slightly faded within the last few years, that is now part of the charm

for Giovanni fans. Pride of performance extends to the kitchen, and Mr. Giovanni is likely to have his own ideas as to what you would enjoy most. But we can put in an advance plug for clam aspic as an appetizer, and wonderful cannelloni made with green pasta.

Cocktails, wines and beer.

All dishes are table d'hôte, with luncheon prices from about $10.00 and dinner prices from about $16.00.

Open from Monday through Friday from noon until 9:30 p.m.

Closed Saturday, Sunday and all major holidays. Also closed August 4th through September 1st.

Reservations recommended.

Jackets required for men.

No credit cards.   PC

★★ GLOUCESTER HOUSE

37 East 50th Street   PL *5-7394*

To the standard menu and preparation of the good-but-not-extraordinary class into which most of New York's fish restaurants fall, Gloucester House adds a sparkling Cape Cod interior more enjoyable than most. That's about it.

Cocktails, wines and beer.

All dishes are à la carte with luncheon and dinner entrées from about $2.50 to $15.50.

Open 7 days a week. Open Monday through Saturday from noon until 10:00 p.m. Open Sunday from 1:00 p.m. until 10:00 p.m.

Closed Thanksgiving and Christmas.

Reservations recommended.

Jacket and tie required.

AE   BA   DC   MC

★★ GOODALE'S

986 Second Avenue (near 52nd Street)   755-7317

A chummy atmosphere is generated at this small fish restaurant by the host-proprietor, who is so proud of his establishment that on a first visit you may feel that the welcome, while genial, includes a degree of inspection, as if you were trying out for membership in a club. It's a club worth joining.

Goodale's strictly U.S.A. cuisine makes you realize how rarely a New York restaurant comes through in this field. The broiled red snapper is a good straightforward affair, as fresh as if the restaurant were really at dockside in Maine, as the décor pretends. With a baked potato, a vegetable, and the salad, the large portion is a good meal.

The real bargain at Goodale's and perhaps the best dish as well, is lobster and scallop stew, good enough to make you think that it's a privilege to be allowed within the doors—an idea that your waiter may share. He doesn't quite say, "You're lucky to be here," but, of course, you are.

Odd, but the salad dressings are execrable.

Cocktails, wines and beer.

The à la carte menu for both lunch and dinner is priced from $2.50 to $11.50.

Open Monday through Friday from noon until 9:20 p.m.

Closed Saturday, Sunday, Christmas, Thanksgiving, New Year's Day and July 4th.

Reservations recommended.

AE   BA   CB   DC

★ HANNIBAL'S STEAK PARLOR

1464 First Avenue (near 76th Street)   861-4214

Here's a lively little joint, a kind of poor man's P. J. Clarke's (which see), junior size, seating 20 comfortably enough at tables, 10 elbow to elbow at the bar, with room left for maybe half a dozen more to stand straight up while waiting.

Up until 6:30 or 7:00 you'll find the place maybe half full, but by 9:00 on a weekend or holiday it may be a seething mass of funlovers. The jukebox will play incessantly. It's part of the atmosphere, like it or not.

Whether you can really call it "dining" is a question, but the thing is, there are not many places where you can get more than acceptable food at Hannibal's prices. The big bargain is the brochette of beef.

Around midnight the jukebox is muted to an unobtrusive level and you'll find a few couples playing backgammon at the bar. In its way, Arcadian.

Cocktails, wines and beer.

Open for dinner only. The à la carte items cost from about $4.50 to $9.50 which includes salad and potato. There is an after-theatre special supper of ribs and steaks from $4.50 to $9.50.

Open 7 days a week from 4:00 p.m. until 2:00 a.m.

Closed Christmas.

No reservations required.

There is a new garden room.

AE   BA   CB   MC

★★★ HOUSE OF TU

322-324 East 44th Street   679-0777

Pick up your menu here and you flounder in what amounts to an inexhaustible list of choices. We counted 146 dishes, and on the basis of those we tried during independent visits and one banquet given by a Chinese acquaintance, we'd like to make a lifework of sampling them all. But if you go only once, begin with the dish listed simply as "Crisp Fish," a whole sea bass deep fried until it has a heavy brown crust, seasoned with fresh scallions and served in a thick puddle of ginger sauce. Although listed on the menu as one of the spicy dishes, it could outrage only the most timorous of palates. We find it just about as good as any fish we've ever eaten.

The House of Tu seats 200 people and is decorated with restraint. Not a wind chime or a red tassel in the place. Prices are at bargain level. If two people choose to make a meal of a single dish, there's an extra charge of $2, but that's still pretty good. And monosodium glutamate, the bugbear of Chinese cooking for allergics, will be omitted from your order if you ask. Also, cornstarch, sugar, and salt can be left out. There are as well five dieter's specials that contain no sugar or cornstarch in the original recipe.

You will find dishes listed here as "ocean flavored." It means prepared with an unlimited number of flavorings. We tried ocean-flavored pork shreds, sautéed with bamboo shoots, ear mushrooms, and garlic, and found it topnotch. Among bland dishes, the velvet chicken, a cross between noodles and fluffy clouds made of finely ground chicken with flour and egg whites, is as delicate as it sounds, and a dish of chicken breast sautéed with fresh watercress and green pepper is also among the leaders. But you can hardly go wrong anywhere here.

Cocktails, wines and beer.

At lunch, à la carte dishes cost from about $2.50 to $4.50. Table d'hôte dinners are from $3.50 to $8.50.

Open 7 days a week from 11:30 a.m. until 11:00 p.m.
Reservations accepted.
Banquet and party facilities are available.
AE   BA   DC

★★★ HUNAM

845 Second Avenue (at 45th Street)   MU 7-7471

Here's at least one Chinese restaurant that advertises a spicy cuisine ("hot, hot, hot") and isn't afraid to serve it. There are also mild dishes for your timorous dinner companion. The restaurant, wildly popular, is divided into two rooms, one kept so dark you can hardly see (although we were able to detect spots on our wine glasses on one occasion) and the other brightly lit. The food is excellent and, everything considered (including the large size of the portions), not at all expensive.

Hunam advertises widely the four-star rating given it some time ago by "New York's Number 1 Newspaper." We disagree with the fourth star because Hunam's popularity hasn't made for a relaxed atmosphere. The waiters perform their duties efficiently but seem terribly worried and hard-pressed in keeping up with the rush. But those spicy dishes, under any circumstances, are great.

Cocktails, wines and beer.

All dishes are à la carte, with main courses at midday from about $2.75 to $4.75; in the evening, from about $3.75 to $7.95.

Open 7 days a week. Open Monday through Thursday and Sunday from 11:30 a.m. until 11:30 p.m.; Friday and Saturday until 1:30 a.m.

Closed Thanksgiving.

Reservations required at lunch, recommended at dinner.
AE   DC

★ HUNAN IN THE VILLAGE

163 Bleecker Street (at Sullivan Street)   *777-1395*

The menu, which is the same for lunch and dinner, lists 20 appetizers and soups, 47 main dishes, 22 vegetables, rices, noodles, and desserts, and a post-scriptual Cantonese menu plus other odds and ends, a grand total of 115. We found that minced chicken corn soup was an excellent beginner (one order served two, easily). The most expensive dish on the menu (at this writing) is a chef's specialty, Dragon and Phoenix, which, at $6.95, is also plenty for two—the dragon being spicy lobster, and the phoenix bland chicken sautéed with snow peas, bamboo shoots, and Chinese mushrooms. A less familiar dish, and very good, is sliced lamb sautéed with scallions.

With most of the portions large enough to share, the food here can be called a bargain. It's an enjoyable place, too—a long narrow room with no pretensions to style but a happy air about it.

Cocktails, wines and beer.

At lunch, table d'hôte costs from about 2.25 to $3.50. Dinner is à la carte with items costing from about $2.50 to $6.95.

Open 7 days a week. Open from noon until 1:00 a.m. Monday through Friday; until 2:00 a.m. on Saturday and Sunday.

Reservations accepted.

AE DC MC

★★ IL GATTOPARDO

45 West 56th Street   586-3978

Il Gattopardo (Italian for Leopard) is small enough to seem a miniature restaurant in comparison with others in the area, and loving attention has been given to making—and keeping—it an attractive spot.

The cooking, too, is imaginative enough to serve as a rebuke to anyone who insists on thinking of Italian cuisine in terms of spaghetti and meat sauce.

Cocktails, wines and beer.

All dishes are à la carte, with main dishes at midday from about $6.00 and up; in the evening, from about $10.00 and up.

Open Monday through Saturday from noon until 10:45 p.m.

Closed Sunday and all major holidays.

Reservations recommended.

AE DC

★★★ IL MONELLO

1460 Second Avenue (between 76th and 77th Streets)
LE 5-9310

Il Monello is a welcome phenomenon, a fairly large restaurant that has not only kept up the high quality of the food and service with increasing popularity, but seems even to have improved. Also, it has an increasingly enthusiastic clientele without having become an "in" place. This is a thoroughly professional yet at the same time a highly personal restaurant, thanks to the kinetic and apparently tireless proprietor, Adi Giovanetti, who comes as close to giving personal attention to every table as is possible.

What to recommend? Well, we love the pastas, including the extremely fine spaghetti called "capelli d'angelo" (angel's hair) marinara, and fettucini "Il Monello," a mixture of green and white. Also the cannelloni, delicate and deliciously herbed. Among the entrées just order your favorite Italian dish, or whatever specialty the waiter recommends. We are fond of paillard of veal or beef (an average-size piece flattened out very thin and lightly grilled) and found the veal especially good here.

"Il Monello" translates, more or less, as "the tough kid" or "the street urchin." By association alone, it could mean "usually a full house, with good reason."

Cocktails, wines and beer.

All dishes are à la carte, with main courses at both lunch and dinner from about $4.40 to $9.00.

Open Monday through Thursday from noon until 11:00 p.m.; Friday and Saturday until midnight.

Closed Sunday, Thanksgiving, Christmas and New Year's Day.

Reservations required at dinner.

AE BA DC MC

★ **IL RIGOLETTO**
232 East 53rd Street   759-9384

Il Rigoletto, which got off to a three-star start, has had so much trouble with ups and downs in the kitchen and a defective air conditioning system, that some of the early patrons abandoned it. At this writing the ventilation has been put in order and things are looking up again.

The kitchen at its best is excellent. We remember especially some seafood hors d'oeuvre (oysters Venetian style, mussels in herbed broth) and we have also enjoyed duck and rabbit—two separate dishes, that is. We will be delighted if you visit Il Rigoletto and decide that you must pencil in another star or two in the margin.

Cocktails, wines and beer.

Table d'hôte lunches are from about $6.95 to $8.50. Dinners are à la carte, with main courses from about $5.25 to $8.95.

Open Monday through Saturday from noon until 10:30 p.m.

Closed Sunday and major holidays.

Reservations recommended.

AE   DC   MC

★ IL VALLETTO
133 East 61st Street   838-3989

Just exactly how can you evaluate a restaurant that can serve you a sublime pasta, a good chicken, and a very ordinary roast of veal? What do you do when the room is attractive, the service efficient and genial, and the kitchen undependable? Il Valletto puts a reporter in an awkward position. About the best way to beat around this bush is to say you'll probably enjoy a visit whether or not you happen to get a break on the food.

It's a pleasant room, not much changed in decoration from that of its former tenant, the pseudo-English country gentry restaurant called The Running Footman. The air is now genuinely New York Italian.

Il Valletto is a large branch off a small parent, Nanni, which is also reported in this book.

Cocktails, wines and beer.

All dishes are à la carte, with main courses at midday from about $4.75 and up; in the evening, from about $6.50 and up. Nanni special every day at $7.50.

Open Monday through Saturday from noon until 11:30 p.m.

Closed Sunday and all major holidays. Also closed from August 4th through Labor Day.

Reservations recommended.

AE   DC   MC   PC

★ INAGIKU

111 East 49th Street (Waldorf-Astoria Hotel)   *355-0440*

The food is authentic enough, the waitresses in Japanese costume are the real article, and the restaurant is efficiently operated. Reservations are honored, and if you don't have one, the bar where you can wait for a table to fall open is luxurious. But "luxurious" brings us down to the nitty-gritty of Inagiku's weak point in comparison with New York's other Japanese restaurants. In spite of its tatami room, Inagiku is more Waldorf-Astoria (it's in that building) than Tokyo. It can get terribly noisy when crowded, and the presentation of the dishes is less artful than it should be at the prices. There is also a certain brusqueness from the male members of the staff that compares unfavorably with traditional Japanese courtesy.

Cocktails, wines and beer.

Table d'hôte luncheons are from $7.00 to $10.00. Table d'hôte dinners are from $8.00 to $22.00; the dinner à la carte menu is priced from about $8.00 to $10.00.

Open 7 days a week. Monday through Thursday noon until 10:00 p.m.; Friday and Saturday until 10:30 p.m. and Sunday until 9:30 p.m.

Closed major holidays.

Reservations required at lunch, recommended at dinner.

Hocho ceremony every Sunday.

AE   BA   CB   DC   MC

★★ INCA BAR & RESTAURANT

399 West 12th Street   *242-9722*

This is an amazingly versatile restaurant with good cooking, low prices, and a bohemian but thoroughly respectable atmosphere stemming from its dockside location and Greenwich Village clientele. At a single meal we've had Spanish gazpacho, Turkish dolmas, Peruvian ceviche, East India curry, and Cuban picadillo, without exhausting the international range of a menu that also includes some plain American broiled fish and conventional seafood dishes—all just about as inexpensive as good food gets in New York. If you are coming by cab, tell your driver you want the very end of West 12th Street, the last building before the docks on the northeast corner. Or you can get off somewhere near and just keep walking westward along well lighted streets.

Cocktails, wines and beer.

Open for dinner only with à la carte dishes costing from about $3.65 to $5.65.

Open 7 days a week from 6:00 p.m. until 12:30 a.m.

Reservations not accepted.

AE   BA

★★ INDIA HOUSE EAST
201 East 34th Street   MU *4-9367*

Because of its more conspicuous location, India House East is always better filled than its uptown-sidestreet offspring, India Pavilion, which we prefer for the very fact of its seclusion. But the parent house has a wider selection of dishes and also a liquor license. You might like it better. The food is, of course, authentically Indian. The service is both informal and very good. The room is small but not small enough to induce claustrophobia and is rather wildly decorated with enlarged approximations of Indian miniature paintings.

Cocktails, wines and beer.

Complete luncheons are from about $1.95 up, with complete dinner from about $4.40 to $6.40.

Open 7 days a week. Open Monday through Friday from noon until 11:00 p.m. Open Saturday and Sunday from 4:00 p.m. until 11:00 p.m.

Closed Saturday and Sunday for lunch; also Thanksgiving.

Reservations recommended.

No credit cards.

★★★ INDIA PAVILION

325 East 54th Street   838-9702

This small restaurant—not exactly a hole in the wall, more like a tunnel—gets a third star on the basis of the purity of its cooking and faith that it won't let us down in that respect, along with its low prices. Also, it's a very nicely decorated little place. It is never crowded. For one thing, it is so inconspicuously located on its side street that people who want to come back often have trouble finding it.

If you're afraid of spicy food we'd suggest you try the biryani, which is lamb and chicken with rice, plentifully herbed but not at all peppery. Both of the Indian breads—the balloon-like puri and the unleavened paratha—are excellent here. Be sure you get a side dish of cucumber and yogurt, especially for cooling off if you order one of the very hot dishes.

Also, try lassi for dessert. Lassi is rosewater and yogurt thinned out to milky consistency, and when it's served you'll think it is hand lotion (honey and almond cream?), but we have yet to meet anyone who, after the first suspicious sip, did not drain the glass to the last perfumed drop.

No liquor. Bring your own wine.

Complete lunch is from $2.25 to $4.95. Complete dinners are from $4.40 to $6.40.

Open Monday through Friday from noon until 11:00 p.m.; Saturday from 4:00 p.m. until 11:00 p.m.

Closed Sunday. Also closed Saturday for lunch and Thanksgiving.

Reservations recommended for dinner.

No credit cards.

★★★ ISLE OF CAPRI

1028 Third Avenue (at 61st Street)   *752-9410*

The Isle of Capri would be many people's choice as the best Italian restaurant in New York and certainly ties for first place with a couple of others on our list of recommendations. It has been enlarged twice since we discovered it 17 years ago and now is much fancier, but the food hasn't suffered a bit.

The restaurant is the creation of Signora Lamanna, who still runs it as if it were her dining room at home. Her pastas and veals have the reputation of being the Isle of Capri's star dishes, but we're even keener on the chicken, and find it impossible to get away from baked clams as an appetizer. Some people to whom we've recommended the place have come back resentfully saying that the portions are too small. Actually that's one thing we like about the Isle of Capri. You aren't stuffed with food, but delighted with encompassable portions beautifully prepared.

There are upstairs and downstairs rooms, the downstairs being the first enlargement. Then the sidewalk tables were permanently glassed in as part of the upstairs room. Take your choice. For old times' sake we sit at one of the old marble-topped tables—which are now covered with snowy white cloths.

Cocktails, wines and beer.

All dishes are à la carte, with main courses at midday from *about $4.50 to $9.50; in the evening, from about $4.75 to $10.00.*

Open Monday through Thursday from noon until midnight; Friday and Saturday until 1:00 a.m.

Closed Sunday, Christmas, New Year's Day, Thanksgiving, July 4th and Labor Day.

Reservations recommended.

AE   CB   DC

★★ ISTANBUL CUISINE

315 Amsterdam Avenue (between 74th and 75th Streets) 874-9773

This tiny place rocks along unnoticed except by Turkish ambassadors, occasional self-effacing movie stars, the staff of the nearby American Museum of Natural History (who told us about it), and some plain people who think that $10-or-so-and-bring-your-own-liquor is the most astounding bargain in town for the kind of food you get here, which is Turkish and unbeatable in its class.

The room is very simple, absolutely immaculate, and the service, carried out by the chef and the owner (who spell one another at the stove and on the floor), is genial.

The only person we know who hasn't responded to this place with delight was a middle-aged lady who walked out in a dudgeon when Hasan, the proprietor, patted her on the shoulder.

If you make up a party of four it will give you an opportunity to sample numerous dishes by dividing them, especially the hors d'oeuvre. You will want to try all of these. After that, the shish kebab village style is not to be missed, and if you want to explore further, leave it to Hasan.

No liquor. Bring your own wine.

The à la carte menu at both lunch and dinner is from about $2.00 to $5.00.

Open Tuesday through Sunday from noon until 11:00 p.m. Closed on Monday.

Reservations recommended.

No credit cards.

★★★ ITALIAN PAVILION
24 West 55th Street   JU 6-5950

After nearly 20 years in its present location, the Italian Pavilion is known to most midtown restaurant buffs, and if ever it has failed any of them, we haven't heard about it. Sit at the bar waiting for your lunch date to arrive and you will notice that nine out of ten people who come in are greeted by name as they are shown to their tables. But this isn't one of those if-you're-not-in-forget-it places. Coming in anonymously from time to time over many years, we have always been beautifully taken care of.

The informal elegance of the Italian Pavilion's front room is one of its first attractions, but there is also a garden room in back, lighter and airier if that's your preference.

Pastas, chicken, and veal are the stars here, with chicken Gismonda (breaded breast on a bed of spinach topped with mushrooms) and veal cutlet alla Magenta (with a flavorsome wine sauce) among our favorites. And for a first-rate midtown restaurant, the prices are not at all exorbitant.

Cocktails, wines and beer.

All dishes are à la carte, with main courses at midday from about $7 to $10; in the evening, from about $10 to $14.00.

Open Monday through Saturday (except summer, see be-

low) from noon until 10:30 p.m.

Closed Sunday, Easter, July 4th, Labor Day, Thanksgiving, Christmas and New Year's Day. Also closed on Saturday during July and August.

Reservations recommended.

AE CB DC

★★ JACQUES'

210 East 58th Street   *753-5513*

The former Tik Tak Hungarian restaurant recently moved from uptown to this fashionable address. The menu now omits three dishes formerly "suggested for weight watchers." Nobody watching his weight would be fool enough to come here, for in spite of its new Frenchified name and its slicked-up quarters, the specialties are still goulashes, paprikas, and schnitzels served in gargantuan portions.

If you go for brains, you can get them here as an appetizer—scrambled with eggs, onions, and paprika. Not for us, however. We chose mushroom fritters with tartare sauce. A single portion served two and could have stretched to three. If you're really crazy about brains, they also come as an entrée.

Jacques' Wiener schnitzels stand up well against memories of their preparation in restaurants specializing in them in their home town, Vienna. There's a braised and roasted veal shank that, although terrifying at first sight, may occupy you happily for a full half-hour of dissection and ingestion. The hashed brown potatoes that come with your entrées are robust and irresistible.

Service is genial and expert. Hungarian wines, unfamiliar in this country, are accompanied on the list with descriptions that help out, and they are interesting to try.

Cocktails, wines and beer.

A la carte entrées at lunch are from $3.25 to $6.95; dinner à la carte dishes are from $5.95 to $8.25. The after-theatre menu is à la carte and ranges from about $3.25 to $7.25.

Open 7 days a week from noon until 3:00 a.m., with after-theatre hours extending until 4:00 a.m.

Reservations recommended at lunch, required at dinner. After-theatre reservations are recommended.

There is a terrace for outdoor dining.

AE   BA   MC

★ JAI-ALAI
82 Bank Street   989-5826

Jai-Alai has failed us a couple of times with brusque service and a bit too much fishy odor in the dining room, but if you are willing to run that risk and don't expect anything like elegance, you might find yourself among this restaurant's list of persistent fans. Jai-Alai claims to have introduced paella to New York, a claim vigorously contested by half a dozen other Spanish restaurants of its vintage. Jai-Alai's portions of this dish, in any case, are gargantuan.

Cocktails, wines and beer.

All dishes are à la carte, with main courses at midday from about $2.00 to $5.00; in the evening, from about $3.75 to $9.00.

Open 7 days a week from noon until midnight; Friday and Saturday until 1:00 a.m.

Reservations accepted.

AE   CB   DC   MC

★ JOE ALLEN
326 West 46th Street   581-6464

Joe Allen's is supposed to be popular with stage and TV people, and although we have never spotted a familiar face there, a likely bunch crowds the bar and dining room. The waiters look like young actors out of a job, and they put on quite a performance as personality kids, as if hoping there's a talent scout among the diners. It's all very informal, quite engaging, and the food, running to hamburgers, chicken pie, and other simple American fare, is not bad at all.

Cocktails, wines and beer.

All dishes are à la carte, with main courses at midday from $2.75 and up; in the evening, from about $3.95 to $4.95.

Open 7 days a week from noon until 2:00 a.m.

Closed Christmas.

Reservations recommended.

MC

★ JOE AND ROSE

747 Third Avenue (between 46th and 47th Streets)
980-3985

This restaurant has been in the same location a long time—since Prohibition days, they say—and refused to sell the property when all around it was being acquired for the construction of a skyscraper, with the result that the skyscraper was built above and embraces it. Although remodeled, the place retains something of the air of an old-timer. There's no menu; the waiter recites to you the day's offerings, which run to steaks, roast beef, pasta, and fish. Everything is good, but relatively expensive.

The trouble with Joe and Rose is that you don't feel really welcome unless you're one of the gang. We have waited half an hour after arriving on time for a reservation, and, seated late, have been rushed out of the place as fast as the waiter could manage it. Not so good. And too bad.

Cocktails, wines and beer.

128

*Special luncheons every day from $5.75 and up; à la carte
dinners begin at $5.75.*

*Open Monday through Saturday from noon until 10:30
p.m.*

*Closed Sunday, major holidays and the first 3 weeks in
July.*

Reservations recommended.

AE   DC

★ **JOHN'S**

302 East 12th Street   GR *5-9531 or 873-4025*

Among the dozens, or maybe hundreds, of
family-style Italian restaurants in New York, John's
has something special in atmosphere that should
please you if you like your Italian food hearty and
inexpensive. The place has been there since 1908, and
the small front room, which used to be the entire
restaurant, is still there to prove it with a handsome
tile floor and a marble dado the likes of which you no
longer find in this age of wallboard. It's a pleasant
spot, with white tablecloths and red napkins and lots
of candles burning atop mounds of drippings in the
traditional semi-bohemian manner.

Portions are so generous that it's a good idea to
share them if you are having more than one course.
Hot eggplant as an appetizer, for instance, smothered
in olives, tomatoes, and mushrooms, is more than any
but a trencherman can manage alone if he expects to
eat anything else. We have enjoyed a meal at John's
for only about $6 a person before tip.

As an added attraction, John's is convenient for
theatregoers headed for the Eden, the Gate, or the
Negro Ensemble Company at the St. Marks Play-
house.

Cocktails, wines and beer.

Open for dinner only with à la carte entrées from about $2.95 to $4.95.

Open from Tuesday through Sunday. Tuesday through Saturday open from 5:30 p.m. until 11:00 p.m.; Sunday from 5:00 p.m. till 9:30 p.m.

Closed Monday, Thanksgiving, Christmas and the month of August.

Reservations recommended.

No credit cards.   PC

★★ KATJA

225 East 58th Street   PL *1-5488*

This is a noisy and expensive restaurant but it has, without question, the first thing it sets out to achieve—flair. There's a glossy quality to everything, including the clientele. In spite of the Russian name, the cuisine is a combination of French and North Italian with Russian fillips including a buffet froid Muscovite spread out in czarist splendor near the entrance. It sure beat anything we were able to find in Moscow not long ago.

All we can say about the food is that the same dish has varied from excellent to only acceptable on different visits. The best thing we had here was a plain, straightforward grilled sole. Among the entrées we liked baked clams in white wine flavored with saffron. The main point of a visit to Katja's, however, is to enjoy a glittery evening, which the place is well equipped to deliver.

Cocktails, wines and beer.

Prix fixe luncheon is $10.00. The à la carte dinner menu is from $8.75 to $16.50.

Open Monday through Saturday (see below) from noon until midnight.

Closed Saturday lunch and all day Sunday. Also closed major holidays and the month of August until after Labor Day.

Reservations recommended.

AE   CB   DC   MC

★★ KEEN'S ENGLISH CHOP HOUSE
72 West 36th Street   WI 7-3616

Although almost obstreperously decorated with mugs, clay pipes, and other paraphernalia in the American Pickwickian Pub Style, this is a pleasantly spacious restaurant running, naturally, to steak, kidneys, even mutton, and other expectables, very well prepared.

Cocktails, wines and beer.

Table d'hôte luncheons are from $5.00 to $11.50. A la carte dinners are from $5.00 to $11.75.

Open 7 days a week, excluding summer weekends (see below), from noon until 11:00 p.m.

Closed summer weekends, July 4th, Labor Day and New Year's Day.

Reservations accepted.

AE   BA   CB   DC   MC

★★★ KITCHO
22 West 46th Street   575-8880

There's another Kitcho (which means Good Luck), much smaller and simpler, at 103 West 44th Street, but this larger branch is the more attractive. Both are always filled with Japanese and if it's authenticity you want first, Kitcho is the place to find it. The larger Kitcho on West 46th seats perhaps a hundred diners, and we have been there when there were no other Westerners present.

They have something called "chef's selection" by which you leave everything up to the kitchen. It is likely to run to 10 or 12 courses, served at proper tempo—unhurried but not sluggish. We ordered sake to go with ours, but noticed that the majority of the Japanese were drinking a replacement that has become popular in Japan—whisky highballs throughout the meal.

The waitresses at Kitcho are helpful in spite of their limited English. On a recent visit, one of them, fearful that we would indulge the American passion for dousing everything with soy sauce, put the lid on the pitcher for one course and said firmly, "No. No soy." Then pointing to our plates she commanded, "Eat!"

We did, with great pleasure.

Cocktails, wines, beer and sake.

Complete luncheons and dinners are priced from $5.00 to $7.50. The à la carte menu is priced from $3.50 and up.

Open Monday through Friday from noon until 10:30 p.m. Open Sunday from 5:00 p.m. until 10:30 p.m.

Closed Saturday, Sunday lunch and all major holidays. Reservations recommended.

AE

★★★ LA BIBLIOTHEQUE

341 East 43rd Street   689-5444

La Bibliothèque may not have the most dramatic site of any New York restaurant—that title would have to be decided by competition among several that occupy the top floors of skyscrapers—but it certainly has one of the prettiest. Its terrace divides the dead end of 43rd Street where it drops off for 30 or 40 feet, from the stairway leading down to First Avenue and a small garden. Sitting on the terrace or at a window table inside, you look across at the main plaza of the United Nations. With one star for the site alone, a total of three is amply justified by the expert kitchen, the service, and a happy atmosphere.

Cocktails, wines and beer.

The à la carte items at lunch cost from about $4.95 to $6.75; table d'hôte is from $4.95 to $9.50. At dinner, à la carte entrées are from $6-$8; with table d'hôte from about $5.25 to $11.95. Pre-theatre special supper is prix fixe at $9.50.

Open Monday through Saturday from noon until mid-night (last order). Pre-theatre supper is from 5:00 until 7:30 p.m.

Reservations recommended.

Pianist nitely from 8:00 until midnight. Outdoor café available for backgammon.

AE BA CB DC MC

★★ LA BONNE SOUPE
48 West 55th Street   586-7650

This is a cross between a bistro and snack bar, and you get as much good food for your money as you are going to find anywhere in New York. "Les hamburgers" as they call them, served with french fries and salad, are large steaks hachés with a variety of sauces.

Living it up (les hamburgers are the least expensive items on the menu) we ordered quenelles de brochet and found this dish, which is difficult to prepare, amazingly good in what is essentially a short-order restaurant. There are fondues, omelets, the soups that give the place its name, and, if you want to aim high, pepper steak. The chocolate fondue with cakes and fruit for dipping is a great dessert.

Naturally, little attention is given to high style at

the very modest prices, but the service is efficient and cheerful. New York could use a Bonne Soupe just around every corner.

Cocktails, wines and beer.

The à la carte lunch and dinner items cost from $2.50 to $8.50. There is a special soup meal including soup, bread, wine and dessert at $3.25.

Open 7 days a week from noon until midnight. Brunch is at 4:00 p.m. on Sunday.

Reservations not accepted.

No credit cards.

★★★★ LA CARAVELLE
33 West 55th Street   JU 6-4252

We are not going to call La Caravelle the best restaurant in New York because we are not going to call any restaurant the best restaurant in New York. But we are going to say that the best restaurant meal we have ever eaten in France was at the Pyramide on New Year's Day, 1953, when that restaurant was generally recognized as the best in France and hence in the world, and the best restaurant meal we have ever eaten in New York was at La Caravelle almost exactly 21 years later.

We have to add immediately that at that time this guide was not projected and we didn't expect to be called on to review La Caravelle. So, with a reservation under our own name, we explained to the management that this was a personal, not a business, visit in celebration of an important anniversary. (It was only coincidentally the anniversary of our great meal in France; that occurred to us later.) Under those circumstances we accepted without qualms the kind of preferential attention that restaurant reviewers who do not work anonymously expect as a matter of course.

This meant an introductory sampling of small portions of a number of specialties rather than a full portion of only a dish or two—including four pâtés, each more delectable than the other, and a divided order of quenelles de brochet, which were unsurpassable. It meant wild (not barnyard) pheasant as the entrée, not on the menu because there were only two birds in the kitchen. (They were brought in for our inspection before preparation, sitting proudly on a silver tray in full plumage. "Oh, I wouldn't have liked that!" some of our friends say. We loved it.) It also meant a gauzy strawberry soufflé for dessert—available to anyone with the foresight to order it. If it meant a special eye on our dishes before they left the kitchen, it didn't make any difference, since preparation at La Caravelle is kept at a uniformly superb level in any case.

Is there a caste system? Some say yes, some say not enough to worry about. Certainly there are tables where distinguished members of the clientele are put on display, and they are worth looking at, harmonizing as they do with the discreet elegance of their setting. Any restaurant that is usually well filled will naturally give regular customers their favorite tables.

The question may arise as to why we retain a fourth star for La Caravelle when we have knocked it off for La Côte Basque, a marvelous restaurant, because it is notorious for playing favorites, and also, more reluctantly, for La Grenouille, which has given us both four-star and three-star experiences. Well, just put it down to confidence that La Caravelle has never served anything less than four-star food in a four-star ambiance and is at least relatively democratic in its treatment of the anonymous, but well-stuffed, wallet.

Cocktails, wines and beer.

Table d'hôte lunch costs $13.75; table d'hôte dinner costs about $20.75.

Open 7 days a week, except summer, from 12:15 until 10:30 p.m.

Closed Saturday and Sunday in summer and all legal holidays. Also closed from July 25th until after Labor Day.

Reservations recommended.

No credit cards.   PC

★ LA CHAUMIERE
310 West 4th Street   741-3374

"Chaumière" means "thatched cottage," and this very pleasant restaurant goes in for a combination of rusticity and cozy provincial charm. Also, like La Petite Ferme, Charlie and Kelly's and Beau Village nearby, it is in one of the very few remaining enclaves of Manhattan that reflect the bourgeois peace and comfort of nineteenth-century New York. This atmosphere makes La Chaumière very much worth a visit even though the kitchen lacks the finesse necessary to live up to the ambitious menu—and the prices. Service and presentation are very good. There's continuous canned music but when not too loud it isn't bothersome since it is well selected.

Wines and beer.

Open for dinner only with à la carte dishes from about $5.75 to $12.00. There is a prix fixe dinner during the week only at $9.00

Open 7 days a week from 6:00 p.m. until 1:00 a.m.

Closed New Year's Day.

Reservations recommended.

136

Classical music Friday and Saturday.
AE DC MC

★★ LA COCOTTE
147 East 60th Street   832-8972
    There's a bar with dining tables for two, a main room as attractive as can be, and beyond that a "garden room," which means a glass-enclosed year-round room surrounded by a hedge. Among the three, it would be difficult to choose a favorite for first prize. The kitchen is less consistent; we've had excellent food (grilled lamb chops with perfect french fries) and food that was barely acceptable (flavorless breast of capon on a bed of flavorless spinach). All told, however, La Cocotte comes off very well, as its popularity no doubt proves.
    Cocktails, wines and beer.
    Table d'hôte luncheons are from $6.50 to $9.75. Complete dinners cost from $8.95 to $14.95, with à la carte dishes from $6.95 to $12.50.
    Open from Monday through Saturday from noon until 10:15 p.m.
    Closed Sunday and all major holidays.
    Reservations recommended.
    AE BA DC MC

★★★ LA COTE BASQUE
5 East 55th Street   688-6525
    This restaurant is so beautiful in its discreet elegance that it is a rebuke to more opulently decorated ones in its class, and so beautifully lit that it makes dimmer interiors seem gloomy and brighter ones seem harsh. As a change from the third-rate

paintings that—often rather pleasantly—-decorate other French restaurants, La Côte Basque has illusion-istic murals by Bernard Lamotte that take you out to the sunny harbors and strands of the restaurant's geographical namesake. Your food comes in looking as beautiful as the room, and the service is elegant as well.

The key to La Côte Basque's personality is that it underplays the very superlatives that account for its long standing as a fine, even a great, restaurant. It does not exactly underplay prices, but if you can stand the tariff, you get your money's worth. Our only reservation about this nearly perfect restaurant is that it is notorious for playing favorites. On the principle that your anonymous dollar should be as good as anyone else's, and that you are going to leave an awful lot of them behind you, we are cutting it down to three stars. But if you can stand the ante and are not intimidated by the possibility of being a stepchild for the evening, don't pass up the beautiful experience of a meal at La Côte Basque.

Cocktails, wines and beer.

Table d'hôte lunch is from $15.25; table d'hôte dinner costs $24.75.

Open from Monday through Saturday, except July and August, from noon until 10:30 p.m.

Closed Sunday and all major holidays. Closed Saturday in August and the first 3 weeks in July.

Reservations recommended.

No credit cards.   PC

★★ LA FAMILLE

2017 Fifth Avenue (near 125th Street)   LE 4-9909

The location far uptown and a total lack of expensive flim-flam account for the low prices at La Famille. Without making an act of it, the kitchen turns out such good Southern dishes as collard greens, spareribs, fried chicken, pig's feet, chit'lins and potato salad, with the requisite corn bread and biscuits ("take two and butter them while they're hot") on the side. New Yorkers are using the term "soul food" for Southern fare but it's nothing new and it's not cabin-in-the-cotton fare either. Scarlett O'Hara might have found all this on the table at Tara more than a hundred years ago.

Cocktails, wines and beer.

A special luncheon, including soup and vegetable, costs $1.95; à la carte dishes cost from $2.95 to $7.50. A la carte entrées at dinner cost from $3.95 to $7.50.

Open 7 days a week. Open for dining from 11:30 a.m. to 11:30 p.m. Monday through Friday. Open Saturday from 4:00 p.m. until midnight; Sunday from 2:00 p.m. until 10:00 p.m. Lounge is open Monday through Saturday from 11:00 a.m. until 4:00 a.m.; on Sunday from 1:00 p.m. until 4:00 a.m.

Reservations accepted.

Lounge entertainment on Friday and Saturday from 9:00 p.m. until 2:00 a.m.

No credit cards.

★★ LA FLEUR

235 East 58th Street   *759-5022*

In an unpretentious way this is one of the prettiest little restaurants in town. As to food and service, it is one of those New York restaurants that seem to be about equally divided between knowledgeable and devoted amateurism and true professionalism—a very nice combination when it works. It usually works at La Fleur, although the waiters sometimes get fussed and the kitchen gets slow when pressed by an unexpectedly crowded evening. When operating at its best level, however, La Fleur is a charmer.

Among appetizers, we've had beautiful crêpes—mushroom or spinach, it would be hard to give first place to either over the other—and excellent clams casino. The chicken dishes were uniformly good—Marsala, Kiev, or just plain grilled. There's a pleasant lightness to the food and we also found the portions just right—neither oversized as in so many restaurants, but not exactly dainty either. The prices are really quite reasonable.

Cocktails, wines and beer.

Table d'hôte lunch is $5.25; table d'hôte dinners cost from $8.25 to $10.75.

Open Monday through Saturday (see below) from noon until 11:00 p.m.

Closed Sunday and lunch on Saturday. Also closed July 4th, Thanksgiving, Christmas and New Year's Day.

Reservations recommended.

AE   BA   CB

★★ LA FRONDE
605 Hudson Street   675-9839

The young woman who suggested that we visit La Fronde described it as a feminist restaurant owned, run, and staffed by women who "just want to see if women can make it on their own." But she added, "My date's comment was that La Fronde is the final proof that a woman's place is in the kitchen." Feminism aside, that would be hard to beat as a comment on the food.

La Fronde is a small place, unpretentious without being exactly simple, and its menu, for so small a kitchen, is remarkable. In addition to such standard items as chicken Marengo (to which they give a very vigorous treatment) there is, of all things, couscous. You don't often find this North African dish outside specialty restaurants, and La Fronde's version might not pass muster with purists, but the steamed grain with a few raisins was authentically fragrant and the sauce, very hot-peppered, was satisfactory.

La Fronde serves a fine fresh leaf spinach with all entrées and the wines are sold at minimum mark-up. The climax of any evening there is a chocolate chestnut cake, an incredible confection that would take first prize anywhere from the Ladies' Aid booth at a country fair to a gastronomical convention. With a mound of whipped cream topping it, it is sheer murder. But what a way to go!

Wines and beer.

Open for dinner only, except for weekend brunch (see below), with à la carte entrées at dinner costing from about $4.25 to $5.50. Brunch costs from $2.75 to $3.95, which includes juice, coffee or tea.

Open Monday through Friday from 5:00 to midnight; Saturday and Sunday 4:00 p.m. until midnight.

Reservations for dinner recommended Friday and Saturday. Not necessary for brunch.

No credit cards.   PC

★★ LA GOULUE
28 East 70th Street   988-8169

La Goulue has gone in and out and back and forth as a favorite spot of the Beautiful People, the Jet Set, and this reporter. We've had excellent food there; then, ordering the same dishes a few weeks later, have found them less satisfactory in preparation. One thing, however, does not change and makes a visit worth recommending: With its etched glass doors between the bar and the dining room proper, with the brass guard rail along the shelf back of the banquettes, with the Art Nouveau wall brackets against gleaming paneling, and a single flower on each table, and the cashier sitting in majesty as she should in her little pen, La Goulue is a perfect reproduction of a typical Parisian restaurant that made its first success early in the century and has refused to get its face lifted. You couldn't find a prettier place to risk a disappointment.

Cocktails, wines and beer.

All dishes are à la carte, with main courses at midday from about $15.00; in the evening, from about $22 to $25.00.

Open Monday through Saturday from noon until 11:30 p.m.

Closed Sunday and all major holidays.

Reservations recommended.

AE   DC

★★★ LA GRENOUILLE
3 East 52nd Street   PL *2-1495*

They say La Grenouille operates on the caste system, and it must be true. In the proper company we have been seated in the entrance showcase. With a reservation under a pseudonym we've been taken to the last table in the back, cuddled up against the entrance to the kitchen. For us, the resultant vista of the field was interesting in a special way, with squadrons of captains, waiters, and busboys expertly deployed, moving fast but never obtrusively, while a couple of Major Generals made regular tours of inspection, very sharp-eyed. But not many people are all that interested in observing the logistics of restaurant operation.

Four stars or three? It hurts a little bit to amputate the fourth, in a restaurant where, among other pleasures, we have been ravished by the enormous bouquets of fresh flowers for which La Grenouille is famous. But it is a place where your experience as an anonymous visitor may be in either the two-star or the four-star bracket, so three is safest.

Cocktails, wines and beer.

Table d'hôte lunch is $13.75. The prix fixe dinner costs $23.75.

Open Monday through Saturday from noon until 10:45 p.m.

Closed Sunday, July 4th, Labor Day, Thanksgiving, Christmas, New Year's Day, Washington's Birthday and Memorial Day. Also closed for 6 weeks summer vacation, approximately from July 24th until September 10th.

Reservations required.

AE

★★ LA GRILLADE

845 Eighth Avenue (at 51st Street)   265-1610

La Grillade is a rather quiet restaurant for dinner but if you arrive for lunch without a reservation you might have to wait as long as 40 minutes at the bar. This isn't the worst fate in the world if you have the time to spare. New Yorkers relaxing while they wait for tables can create an engaging atmosphere, and a crowded restaurant usually means good food.

It does at La Grillade, which is every bit as French as its name. The greeting at La Grillade is delightful, the service efficient and friendly, and the general atmosphere a long, long way from Eighth Avenue—

143

about 3,000 miles, or whatever the width of the Atlantic is. On Sunday nights La Grillade becomes a discothèque, but we are unable to report on that.

They do lamb beautifully here, lovely and pink, and we remember also a crêpe maison, listed among the hors d'oeuvre but large enough to have served as a main course, that turned out to be seafood with the accent on scallops and was absolutely first-rate.

Cocktails, wines and beer.

The à la carte luncheon menu is priced from about $3.35 to $9.95; table d'hôte is $4.65. The table d'hôte dinner costs from about $9.75 to $9.95; with à la carte dishes from $6.25 to $17.95.

Open 7 days a week, except summer, from noon until 11:30 p.m.

Closed on Sunday from June to 15th of September and the whole month of August. Also closed July 4th, Christmas, New Year's Day and Memorial Day.

Reservations recommended.

AE   BA   DC   MC

★★   L'AIGLON

13 East 55th Street   PL *3-7295*

The best dish we have sampled here is one of the specialties, veal chop à L'Aiglon, which is topped with a creamy cheese sauce. Oysters Rockefeller also pleased us. We were wondering whether the restaurant could perhaps edge up into the three-star class when our dessert came—zabaglione, thick and gummy, the worst we have ever been served, which we discarded after a few tentative spoonfuls. The charge remained on the check even though the captain had asked what was the matter with it and we had said it was just plain awful. A small thing to wipe out a possible third star? Perhaps, but indicative of a certain loss of style and courtesy in a rather expensive restaurant of long standing. At lunch, however, L'Aiglon is several times as attractive, filled with handsome, well-dressed people. Very New York.

Cocktails, wines and beer.

Complete luncheon costs $9.25, with à la carte dishes from $6.75 and up. Table d'hôte dinners are from $13.25 to $15.75, with à la carte entrées starting at $7.50.

Open 7 days a week from noon until 11:00 p.m.

Closed July 4th, Labor Day, Thanksgiving, Christmas and New Year's Day.

Reservations recommended.

AE   CB   DC   MC

★★ LAIR, THE

70 East 56th Street   751-7321

The best thing about The Lair, which goes in for Frenchish cuisine, is that the staff members really seem to be engrossed in the job of running a good restaurant and making you happy without trying to buddy you up. It doesn't quite seem a professional, commercial restaurant—although to call it amateurish would be an injustice. There are many nice touches—delicate croissants still warm from the oven instead of plain bread, glasses whisked away at the last moment for moderate chilling if you are having white wine (and if you like your glasses chilled).

The Lair is proud of its quiches, and rightly so. We had one with fresh asparagus that was remarkable, the pastry tender and flaky, the custard neither too soft nor too firm.

Cocktails, wine and beer.

All dishes are à la carte, with main courses at midday from

145

about $3.50 to $6.95; in the evening, from about $5.50 to $11.00. The after-theatre menu is priced from $3.50 to $11.00.

Open 7 days a week, except summer, from noon until 1:00 a.m.

Closed on Sunday from Memorial Day to Labor Day and all major holidays.

Reservations accepted but not preferred.

AE   CB   DC   MC

★★ LA MAISON JAPONAISE

334 Lexington Avenue (at 39th Street)   MU 2-7375

"French cooking with an Oriental accent," it says on this restaurant's card, and it does manage sometimes to combine the best of two worlds, or at least to modify a possible defect in one by applying a virtue of the other. If you get a little tired of the generally soft texture of French food you'll welcome the crispness of the vegetables, very lightly sautéed bamboo shoots, bean sprouts and snow peas, that accompany your entrée. There's a touch of soy sauce in the house salad dressing.

There are dishes as purely French as sole amandine and as purely Japanese as tempura, as well as a "curried pork à la Japonaise" that struck us as being more Indonesian than anything else. And what nationalities, exactly, would you give brandy Alexander chiffon pie and cream of avocado soup? They're all good.

On the debit side, La Maison Japonaise is noisy and most of the tables are paired so closely that unless you get one of the few small ones arranged in single file along one side of the narrow aisle, you are virtually sharing a table with strangers. (There's a very small, somewhat quieter room upstairs.) Altogether, however, La Maison Japonaise is one of a kind in its mixture of well prepared off-beat dishes at reasonable prices in an engaging atmosphere to which the service, brisk and cheerful, contributes.

Cocktails, wines and beer.

A la carte lunch and brunch costs from about $3.50 to $4.25 and includes salad and coffee. At dinner, the à la carte dishes cost from about $3.95 to $6.95 and include salad, vegetables and rice or noodles.

Open from Sunday through Friday from noon until 10:30 p.m. Sunday brunch is from noon to 3:00 p.m.

Closed Saturday for lunch and major holidays.

Reservations recommended.

AE MC

★★ LA PETITE FERME

189 West 10th Street   242-7035

Getting into La Petite Ferme for a meal is just one degree less difficult than waiting to be invited. The restaurant is so small and has become so famous that you might have to reserve many days in advance unless you have the luck to coincide with a cancellation.

Once you get there you are not going to have any impression that you have been invited to dine with a family at their "petite ferme" somewhere in the countryside. The stage is very cleverly set, however, and in spite of its long-standing success, this little place retains the air of a hobby operated for friends of the chef. Rather fancy friends, for the most part.

Wines and beer.

A la carte lunch for two is from about $25.00 to $35.00; à la carte dinner for two is from $35.00 to $45.00.

Open Tuesday through Sunday for two sittings: lunch at 12:30 and 2:30 and dinner at 7:00 and 9:30 p.m.

Closed Monday, the month of July and all major holidays.

Reservations are recommended for lunch; required for dinner.

No major credit cards. PC

★★★ LA PETITE MARMITE

5 Mitchell Place (just off 49th Street and First Avenue)
826-1084

If you ever get to feeling (as we do) that maybe the French formula for the ideal restaurant is over-praised, La Petite Marmite may bring you back (as it did us) to admitting that, after all, the formula is hard to beat. This is a really delightful spot with banquettes and tables arranged in a way that combines the pleasure of sufficient privacy with the pleasure of watching other people; the service is efficient without being impersonal, personal without being obtrusive. There is no music to make people raise their voices, with the result that this is a quiet place without being at all a dead one. And the cooking—completely French, of course—is first-rate. Want anything more?

Cocktails, wines and beer.

All dishes are à la carte, with main courses at midday from about $4.00; in the evening, from about $6.75 and up.

Open Monday through Thursday from noon until 10:00 p.m. On Friday and Saturday (except summer, see below), open until 11:00 p.m.

Closed Sunday and all major holidays. Closed Saturday from Memorial to Labor Day.

Reservations required at lunch; recommended for dinner.
AE   CB   DC   MC

★★ LA POULARDE

1047 Second Avenue (near 55th Street)   838-2970

La Poularde is the very type of "little French restaurant" that used to be the glory of New York until decimated by present operating expenses, union friction, and the disappearance of chef's apprentices. La Poularde itself very nearly succumbed under the pressure of sudden popularity when favorable notices brought it out of the quiet, leisurely pace it had maintained for six years under the proprietors, Monsieur and Madame Pierrot, who did everything for themselves, Monsieur in the kitchen and Madame doing the honors for the few clients in the dining room.

At present things have calmed down at La Poularde so that Madame doesn't have to lock the door as, for a while, she used to when things got too tight. Monsieur Pierrot still complains that he doesn't have time to make his quenelles de brochet as he used to—and the loss to diners is great.

The restaurant is very simple in décor; no energy is wasted on froufrous, although waitresses have been added to the staff. The menu is brief and the cost moderate. There's not much point in going into detail about individual dishes—except that you should hope for a day when it has been possible to make the quenelles—because everything is good. The food in general is on the rich side, which you expect, when you know that the Pierrots come from Lyons.

Cocktails, wines and beer.

The à la carte luncheon prices begin at $4.50, which is the minimum. Table d'hôte dinners are from about $8.00 to $13.50.

Open Monday through Saturday, except summer, from noon until 9:30.

*Closed Sunday, the month of August and all major holi-
days. Also closed on Saturday from June through August.
Reservations recommended.
AE   MC*

★ LA ROTISSERIE

153 East 52nd Street   759-1685

La Rotisserie falls short of evoking nostalgic
memories of eating experiences in Paris. It is too big
to be called a bistro or to offer any approximation of
the leisure and delight of a meal in that modest restaurant you discovered and made your own on your first
trip to France. Nor does its size generate the excitement of a big, fancy restaurant. But it has virtues, with
the primary one that prices have been kept reasonably
low for authentically French food.

Cocktails, wines and beer.

*The à la carte menu, at both lunch and dinner, is priced
from about $2.95 to $6.50.*

Open 7 days a week from noon until 11:00 p.m.

Reservations recommended.

AE

★ LARRE'S FRENCH RESTAURANT

50 West 56th Street   247-8980

Larré's probably deserves a second star on the
basis of its moderate prices for consistently good food,
but it might be misleading. This is neither a stylish
nor an imaginative restaurant but it turns out good
food so consistently in so French a manner that many
a visiting Frenchman who can afford fancier fare goes
to Larré's just to feel at home.

Cocktails, wines and beer.

The club luncheon (no appetizer) costs from about $2.85 to

$4.50. *Table d'hôte dinner is from $5.25 to $8.25; à la carte from $3.95 to $6.50.*

Open Monday through Saturday from 11:30 until 9:30 p.m.
Closed Sunday.
Reservations for 5 or more only.
AE

★★ LA TOQUE BLANCHE
359 East 50th Street   PL *5-3552*

La Toque Blanche is an old-timer from away back that has always maintained a good level and is currently engaged in a vigorous effort to make it even higher. The service here is the best we have ever found in a restaurant of La Toque Blanche's class—that is, a restaurant of high quality without pretensions to chic or exquisite refinements. The food, with a strong Provençal accent, is more hearty than subtle, and the general atmosphere is appropriately friendly and provincial. Edging up toward three stars, La Toque Blanche may well make the grade.

Cocktails, wines and beer.
All dishes are table d'hôte, with lunch costing about $7.90 and dinner about $11.80.
Open 7 days a week from noon until 11:00 p.m.
Closed all major holidays.
Reservations recommended.
AE DC MC

★★ LE ALPI
234 West 48th Street (between Broadway and Eighth Avenue)   JU *2-7792*

This is easily a three-star restaurant when it isn't too busy. Orders are individually prepared, and, when possible, completed in their final stages at your table. Our two stars are only precautionary. Among the best dishes are boned chicken breasts with rosemary, and veal scaloppine dusted with Parmesan cheese and delicately herbed. These, like the menu in general, are in the best North Italian tradition.

Cocktails, wines and beer.

A la carte entrées at lunch cost from about $4.50 to $7.75. Complete dinner is about $9.00, with à la carte entrées priced from about $4.50 to $7.75.

Open from Monday through Saturday from noon until midnight.

Closed Sunday and all major holidays.

Reservations recommended at lunch; accepted at dinner.

AE CB DC MC

★★ LE BEAU PERE

13 Eighth Avenue (near 12th Street)   *741-8025*

In spite of its French name, Le Beau Père describes itself as a Rumanian restaurant. The atmosphere and décor are colorful merging into the exotic. Your waiter may have his shirt open down to his navel with golden lockets artfully entangled in his chest hair, if that kind of thing bothers you. But the service is good—taking for granted that you expect to wait a while for dishes individually prepared, as these are.

There's no timidity in this kitchen. The sauce on the duck à l'orange, one of several non-Rumanian but Rumanianized dishes, is really full of orange, and the pui cu mujdel leaves no question as to the appropriateness of the name, which means chicken baked in garlic sauce. But the hand that does the flavoring isn't heavy, just enthusiastic, and the dishes come in looking like carnival floats. We mean that as a compliment. Portions are very generous. The imaginative salads can be meals in themselves.

Conjoined with Le Beau Père is a diminutive side-kick, La Belle Mère, a café that takes over into the wee hours after the restaurant proper closes. It has a limited menu based on the big one.

No liquor. Bring your own wine.

Open for dinner only with à la carte entrées priced from about $5.00 to $18.00 After-theatre dishes are from about $1.85 to $10.00.

Open 7 days a week from 6:00 p.m. until midnight. The café is open from 9:00 p.m. until 6:00 a.m., with drinking ceasing at 4:00 a.m.

Reservations accepted.

AE BA DC MC

★ **LE BEC FIN**
232 East 58th Street   741-8025

This is a good straight-down-the-line French restaurant that aims to please and usually does. If you want relief from all those French sauces, you will find it in Escalope de Veau Bec Fin, a thin, lightly breaded cutlet, which came with a twin in our order, both of large size. A hefty and hungry-looking young man at the next table asked what it was and ordered it, but had what looked like only one on his plate—too bad, since one of ours went back to the kitchen.

A pepper steak, richly sauced, was also satisfactory at Le Bec Fin. Smoked salmon, at a stiff supplemental charge on the hors d'oeuvre list, was disappointingly salty.

Unfortunately Le Bec Fin has a bad reputation as a place where you are likely to be hurried out of the place in order to speed up turnover. It hasn't been our experience, but complaints on that score have been numerous.

Wines and beer.

Complete luncheons are priced from about $5.25 to $8.50. Table d'hôte dinners cost from about $8.95 to $11.50.

Open from Monday through Friday from noon until 10:00. Saturday open from 6:00 p.m. until 11:00.

Closed Sunday and all major holidays. Also closed Saturday for lunch.

Reservations recommended.

No credit cards.

★★ LE BOEUF A LA MODE

539 East 81st Street   RH *4-9232*

This is a table d'hôte restaurant whose reputation for consistently good food has been confirmed to the extent that we have been able to test it. It's an attractive place, with an air of professionalism that doesn't pretend to high style. A little bit out of the way, it is something of a neighborhood restaurant patronized by regulars, but it is definitely worth the trip.

If the soup du jour happens to be cream of leek the day of your visit, you are in luck. It could hardly have been improved on the time we had it. Also, very good crabmeat crêpe, served piping hot, is remembered with great pleasure. A duck with cherries was a little dry, but the very good cherry sauce helped out. And the veal Dijonnaise, in a light mustard sauce, was excellent.

Cocktails, wines and beer.

Open for dinner only. The table d'hôte dinners cost from about $7.50 to $11.50.

Open from Tuesday through Sunday from 5:30 to 11:00 p.m.

Closed Monday, the month of August and all major holidays.

Reservations required.

AE   BA   DC

★★ LE CHAMBERTIN
348 West 46th Street   PL *7-2154*

This restaurant has disappointed us now and then—once, for instance, with a roast leg of lamb, although by reputation it is one of the best dishes here—but it manages to maintain an average of such quality in relation to its prices that an occasional fault can be condoned. Le Chambertin is exceptional, also, in its extensive wine cellar with trustable recommendations, on the menu, of the best inexpensive choices. Cheeses and desserts (with tarts as the stars) are excellent.

Le Chambertin is a theatre district restaurant and you're asked to order by six o'clock if you expect to make a 7:30 curtain. We mention this because some otherwise reasonable people are utterly impossible in their demands for pre-theatre service.

We have found Le Chambertin a lively place for lunch, and a very quiet one for dinner after the theatre crowd has cleared out.

Cocktails, wines and beer.

All dishes are table d'hôte, with prices at midday from about $4.25 to $7.00; in the evening, from about $7.00 to $11.00.

Open Monday through Saturday from noon until 9:15 p.m.

Closed Sunday, the month of July and all major holidays.

Reservations recommended.

AE

★★ LE CHANTECLAIR

18 East 49th Street   PL *5-7731 and* EL *5-8998*

René Dreyfus, who with his brother Maurice owns Le Chanteclair, was a European racing car driver during the 1930's and his restaurant at lunchtime is a hangout for motorcar buffs of all kinds, including, for instance, the membership of the American Bugatti Club. You can also spot publishers, agents, and TV people, all being convivial and arranging deals at the bar or over the tables. In the other phase of its schizoid personality, Le Chanteclair becomes a quiet French restaurant for dinner.

The shrimp with garlic are so good here that we sometimes take a double order of this appetizer as an entrée, but we have also enjoyed the lemon sole. The dinner menu is more extensive and fancier than the lunch, and includes two specialties that the chef is justly proud of—a feuilleté au Roquefort and a côte de veau with morilles or cèpes, depending on their availability.

If it's a lively crowd you want, typically New York, try lunch. For a leisurely time in pleasant surroundings, try dinner.

Cocktails, wines and beer.

Table d'hôte lunch is from $6.50 to $10.50. Table d'hôte dinner is from $7.95 to $15.50; à la carte entrées from about $5.25 to $12.50. There is a pre-theatre dinner special at $6.50.

Open Monday through Friday from noon until 9:45 p.m.; Saturday from 5:00 p.m. to 10:30 p.m. The pre-theatre special is served from 5:00 to 7:00 p.m.

Closed Sunday, the first 3 weeks in July and all major holidays.

Also closed Saturday for lunch.

Reservations recommended for lunch; accepted for dinner.
AE   BA   CB   DC   MC

★ **LE CHEVALIER**

1464 Second Avenue (between 76th and 77th Streets)
288-9031

    The people at Le Chevalier still had a lot to learn about running a restaurant when last we visited it, but they were showing promise of growing up. We remember one dish, veal Florentine, sautéed, placed on a bed of spinach, and topped with melted cheese, that was excellent.

    The décor of Le Chevalier is extraordinary, fully worth a visit from any history of art student. An analysis of the combination of styles, running from motel dee-lux to something that can be described only as Jacobean Art Nouveau, would make a great term paper.

*   Cocktails, wines and beer.*
*   Lunch costs from about $3.50 to $5.50; dinner is from $7.95 to $9.75. Both include soup, salad, vegetable and potato.*
*   Open 7 days a week from noon until 11:00 p.m.*
*   Reservations accepted.*
*   There is live entertainment at dinner.*
AE   BA   DC   MC

★ **LE CIRQUE**

58 East 65th Street   794-9292

    Le Cirque has a four-star look, a four-star clientele, and four-star ambitions, but to the extent of our acquaintance, has risen only to one-star performance. Oh, you might add a second for the looks of the place, but you also stand a good chance of getting a bad table where you can't see anything. We have had a grilled boned saddle of lamb here that was delectable, a seafood crêpe that was an excellent filling inside a tough pancake, an excellent Carpaccio (tissue-thin raw beef with a dab of salsa verde on the side), and deplorable veal scaloppine. We've also had spotty wine glasses and inattentive service. Well, it's up and down. Maybe you'll hit Le Cirque when it's up. In any case, it's a very pretty place to sit and wait for service. You can always watch the maitre d'hotel and captains playing up to their favorite guests—which may be why they call this place "The Circus." No other reason is apparent.

Cocktails, wines and beer.

Although there is an à la carte menu, the prix fixe luncheon costs about $9.75. At dinner, à la carte entrées cost from about $7.75 to $12.50.

Open Monday through Saturday from noon until 10:30 p.m.

Closed Sunday and all major holidays.

Reservations recommended.

AE DC

★★★ LE COLISEE
36 East 6oth Street   421-8151

Winds, tides, and the fortunes of Air France are included over and above the normal hazards of restaurant operation for Le Colisée, which specializes in such delicacies as langoustine, turbot, and loup-de-mer flown in daily, or as daily as possible. But there are also such home-grown delicacies as Maine lobster and good American sea bass—the latter not at all a bad substitute for loup-de-mer in one of the best dishes here, a whole fish grilled with fennel and blazed at your table with Pernod. (There is steak for your dinner partner who doesn't like fish.)

The cooking is, at the moment of writing about this brand-new restaurant, quite wonderful. The décor, which simulates the interior of a private yacht, is pleasant and unobtrusive. The chances are that Le Colisée will settle down as a four-star restaurant, but during its proving period, three is safest.

Cocktails, wines and beer.

All dishes are à la carte, with main courses at midday from about $5 to $12.50; in the evening, from about $6 to $16.00.

Open Monday through Saturday from noon until 10:30 p.m.

Reservations recommended.

Closed Sunday and all major holidays.

AE   DC   MC

★★★★ **LE CYGNE**

53 East 54th Street   PL *9-5942*

Le Cygne—the Swan—is well named if the intention is to imply grace and elegance. Its size (rather small for a swan) is doubled by a mirrored end wall, with photomurals enlarged from a perspective map of eighteenth-century Paris at the sides. A spectacular bouquet at the entrance is echoed by pretty flowers on the tables. We have found the food excellent, including a superior selection of cheeses, but our real reason for putting a fourth star up there is the service as the final touch to the extraordinarily pleasant atmosphere of the place.

It is indeed an odd circumstance when you must feel grateful for being well served in an expensive restaurant, but that's the way it is in New York. On our first and anonymous visit, both our captain and our waiter seemed really concerned that this party of four, not very fancy looking, should enjoy both the meal and being expertly cared for, but at the same time they avoided being overly solicitous. Let's hope you get the same treatment.

Cocktails, wines and beer.

The prix fixe luncheon is $12.00; in the evening it is $18.75.

*Open Monday through Friday from noon until 10:30 p.m.
Saturday open from 6:00 p.m. until 11:00 p.m. (except July,
see below).*

*Closed Sunday, the month of August and all major holi-
days. Closed Saturday for lunch; also closed Saturday all day
during July.*

Reservations recommended.

Men are required to wear jacket and tie.

AE   DC

★★ LE FONTAINEBLEAU

*998 Second Avenue (between 52nd and 53rd Streets)
752-8088-9*

This is a small restaurant with a limited menu
that seems to work better at dinner than at lunch, for
some reason. (Or maybe we just had bad luck at
lunch.) At relatively moderate prices, Le Fontainebleau serves unusually good food that immediately
declares the presence in the kitchen of an imaginative chef. The restaurant is jointly owned by the
chef and the man out front, and they care. We've enjoyed everything we have eaten here, but the chicken
with whisky sauce stands out as the most pleasant
memory. Recommended, in spite of an inconsistent
history.

Cocktails, wines and beer.

*All dishes are table d'hôte, with midday prices from $5.00
to $7.00. In the evening, table d'hôte dinner costs from about
$7.50 to $11.00.*

*Open Monday through Friday from noon until 10:30;
Saturday until 11:00.*

Closed Sunday.

Reservations recommended.
AE

★ LE LAVANDOU
134 East 61st Street   838-7987

This new French restaurant makes a point of attractive presentation and is very good at it. The room itself is very pretty, bouquets on the tables are nicely arranged, the table settings are gracious, and when your food is set down before you it looks as if it had just been arranged for photographing for the cover of a food magazine. At this writing the kitchen is not quite as consistently good as the presentation. A rack of lamb was superb, a crabmeat cocktail deplorable. Another star or two will have to wait, but might very well be deserved soon.

Cocktails, wines and beer.

All dishes are table d'hôte, with luncheon prices from about $6.50 to $10.00; in the evening from about $11.50 to $14.50.

Open from Monday through Saturday from noon until 10:00 p.m.

Closed Sunday and all major holidays.

Reservations recommended.

AE

★★★ LE MADRIGAL
216 East 53rd Street   355-0322

From the front door right on back to a little room giving onto what passes for a garden in New York restaurants, this is as pretty a restaurant as you will find in the city. Service is excellent and so is the food. If you like fish and licorice, the striped bass flambé Madrigal, served for two, should be your first choice—a large fish beautifully cooked and then set afire at your table with Pernod. Although popular with a rather fancy crowd, Le Madrigal isn't one of those places that virtually require a social visa for entrance.

Cocktails, wines and beer.

All dishes are à la carte, with main courses at midday from about $5.00 to $11.00; in the evening, from about $8.75 to $15.00.

Open Monday through Friday from noon until 11:00 p.m. Open Saturday from 6:00 until 11:00 p.m.

Closed Sunday and all major holidays. Also closed Saturday for lunch.

Reservations recommended for lunch and dinner; required for after-theatre supper.

AE

★ LE MARMITON
216 East 49th Street   MU 8-1232

Le Marmiton is a typical French restaurant straight down the intimate-bourgeois line. It presents a strong feeling of solidarity among the staff (which provides excellent service) extending to the unseen members in the kitchen—and including, for that matter, a good percentage of the diners, who have the air of seasoned regulars. Feeling very much at home, they apparently don't demand miracles from the kitchen—fortunate, since none are delivered. Special attention is given the wines; there are excellent ones at moderate prices. All in all, however, the best thing Le Marmiton has to offer is the warm, friend-of-the-family atmosphere, and it offers it in abundance.

Cocktails, wines and beer.

Table d'hôte lunch is $6.75 and up; with complete dinner

from $9.00 and up. Special pre-theatre dinner at $7.75.

Open Monday through Saturday from noon until 10:30 p.m. Pre-theatre dinner from 5:00 to 7:00 p.m.

Closed Sunday and all major holidays.

Reservations recommended.

All major credit cards.

★★ LE MISTRAL

14 East 52nd Street   421-7588 and 421-7589

The mistral is a violent wind that sweeps through the valley of the Rhône from time to time. When its namesake restaurant is busy (which is most of the time), you would think the mistral had hit it from the direction of the kitchen, cutting straight through to the checkroom. Blown hither and yon, the waiters are engaged in perpetual scrimmage in the corridor between tables in the restaurant's lower half. It doesn't make for restful dining.

With a prix fixe and a wine list that put it in the bracket of New York's top luxury restaurants, with a décor modeled on their formula, with an obvious acquaintance with how those restaurants are run, and with the best of intentions, Le Mistral nevertheless achieves only an acceptable approximation of their service and cuisine.

Cocktails and wines.

Prix fixe lunches cost $13.75; prix fixe dinners are $20.75.

Open Monday through Saturday from noon until the last order taken at 10:55 p.m.

Closed Sunday and all major holidays.

Reservations required.

AE   DC

★ LE MOAL
942 Third Avenue   688-8860

Averaging the four aspects of a restaurant that we try to balance in rating it—food, price, service, and ambiance—we found Le Moal wanting in all but ambiance on the last of our several visits, and decided to omit it, starless, from this guide. But it must be better than it seems, since it has a steady, loyal clientele. So, on the basis of virtues hidden from us but apparent to them, a star.

Cocktails, wines and beer.

At lunch, table d'hôte is from $5.10 to $7.00. The à la carte menu at dinner is priced from about $5.25 to $7.75.

Open 7 days a week. Open Monday through Saturday from noon until 11:00; Sunday from 1:00 p.m. until 10:00 p.m.

Closed Thanksgiving, Christmas and New Year's Day. Reservations recommended.

AE   DB   DC   MC

★★ LE MUSCADET
987 Third Avenue (near 59th Street)   371-9598

Le Muscadet has the cozy air cherished by lovers of That Little French Restaurant, and has it authentically. The menu is standard, devoid of surprise, and so is the cooking, but it's the kind of food you used to get in the average inexpensive Paris restaurant back in the day—oh, 20, 30 years ago—when it was still true that you couldn't find a really bad meal in that town.

The complete meal, at prices listed here, includes hors d'oeuvre, soup, entrée, dessert, and coffee or tea, with an occasional supplementary charge for certain items—such as a dollar extra if you want coquilles St. Jacques as as appetizer. We did, and found them excellent.

Good food in generous quantities, well served in a sufficiently attractive room, is rare enough to make Le Muscadet a pretty good bargain.

Cocktails, wines and beer.

Lunch is table d'hôte and costs from about $4.50 to $6.75. Table d'hôte dinner is from about $6.75 to $12.00; with à la carte entrées priced from $5.75 to $10.00.

Open Monday through Saturday from noon until 10:00 p.m., Friday and Saturday until 11:00 p.m.

Closed Sunday.

Reservations recommended.

AE

★★ L'ENTRECOTE

1057 First Avenue (between 57th and 58th Streets)
755-0080

One Friday night at this small French steak house we asked the harassed young woman who was taking care of our table if the restaurant was open for lunch. "No—thank God," she said cheerfully. She was young, slender, and vigorous or she would never have made it back to the kitchen through the crowd. During the week it is less crowded, but the steady patronage accorded L'Entrecôte over the years is evidence of its consistently good food. Also of its informal tête-à-tête atmosphere. You are tête-à-tête with your neighbors as well as your dinner partner sometimes, but it's still pretty nice.

Without going into detail, let's just say that the steak and chicken and fish on the brief menu are very well prepared in the manner of a good, but not fancy, French kitchen. And that's good enough.

Cocktails and wines.

Open for dinner only. Prix fixe dinners are from about

$7.50 to $9.50. A la carte appetizers cost from about $1.50 to $2.90.

Open 7 days a week from 6:00 p.m. until midnight.
Closed all major holidays.
Reservations accepted.
AE   MC

★★ LE PERIGORD
405 East 52nd Street   PL *5-6244*

Le Perigord can hardly be described as a simple restaurant, but it is less pretentious than its offspring, Le Perigord Park (see below) and has held up a lot better. Service has had occasional lapses into snootiness, but the worst offender among the captains has gone elsewhere. In general the food is well prepared and nicely presented. The ambiance is agreeably— that is, not aggressively—elegant in a modest way.

Cocktails, wines and beer.
The prix fixe menu at lunch is $9.00; at dinner it's $15.00.
Open Monday through Saturday from noon until 11:00 p.m. (Last order taken at 10:30 p.m.).
Closed Sunday, July 4th, Thanksgiving, Christmas and New Year's Day.
Reservations recommended.
AE

★ LE PERIGORD PARK
575 Park Avenue (at 63rd Street)   *752-0050*

This is one of New York's group of prematurely middle-aging luxury restaurants that have let themselves go. The air of elegance now has an almost nostalgic quality about it; neither the kitchen nor the service really pleases one-time fans who return, apparently, out of habit or pleasant memory. Our own recollections of Perigord Park in its heyday being that it was never quite what it was cracked up to be, we aren't surprised.

Cocktails, wines and beer.

All dishes are table d'hôte, with lunch priced from $10 and up; dinner from $15.00.

Open 7 days a week from noon until 11:00 p.m.

Closed 4th of July, Labor Day, Christmas and New Year's Day.

Reservations recommended.

AE

★ LE PONT NEUF

212 East 53rd Street   751-0373

This is an ambitious small restaurant with an extensive menu and wine list, and all the right ideas about what a French restaurant should be. What it lacks is the flair and style of the restaurants it aspires to emulate. On the other hand, it has an engaging intimacy that they lack—so there you are.

Cocktails, wines and beer.

Complete lunch is priced from about $6.50 to $7.50. The à la carte items at dinner cost from about $10 to $12.00.

Open Monday through Saturday from noon until 10:30 p.m.

Closed Sunday, the first 2 weeks in July and all major holidays.

Reservations recommended.

AE DB DC MC

★ LE POULAILLER

43 West 65th Street   799-7600

On our last visit to Le Poulailler we felt like getting up from our banquette and going out to the kitchen to spank somebody—or everybody. Our otherwise excellent mussels in mustard sauce were salty, and our otherwise excellent billi-bi was downright briny. A very good chicken was smothered in a bland cream sauce that was supposed to have been sorrel sauce, but whoever had had a heavy hand with the salt seemed to have had none at all when it came to the sorrel. There just wasn't any. Our fresh fruit salad was indeed fresh, but very little of it was ripe—and this in midsummer. On the strength of its attractive quarters, its past record, its proximity to Lincoln Center, and the possibility that this last visit was an exception, Le Poulailler squeaks into this book with one star—but it's a concession.

Cocktails, wines and beer.

A la carte entrées at lunch begin at $5.25 and up. Table d'hôte dinners are about $12.75. The after-theatre menu is à la carte and begins at $4.00.

Open Monday through Saturday from noon until 10:30 p.m.

Closed Sunday, the month of August and all major holidays.

Reservations recommended at lunch; required at dinner.
AE DC

★★ LE PROVENCAL
21 East 62nd Street   TE *8-4248*

      Le Provençal is one of New York's sturdiest institutions, with a clientele that, by the looks of it, has entered a happy and prosperous middle age along with the restaurant. Service is attentive but not fawning, and the décor seems calculated to be unobtrusive —and succeeds, in a conventional brownish way. The wine list is very good, with excellent choices at moderate prices. The menu holds no surprises, but the kitchen produces no disappointments. In a contest for "Least swinging French restaurant" Le Provençal would win in a walk—and that is meant as an accolade.

Cocktails, wines and beer.

Table d'hôte lunch is from about $6.00 to $8.75; table d'hôte dinner is from $9.75 to $14.00.

Open Monday through Friday from noon until 10:00; Saturday until 10:30 p.m.

Closed Sunday, the month of August and all major holidays.

Reservations recommended.

AE   BA   MC

★ **LE RABELAIS**
625 Columbus Avenue (between 90th and 91st Streets)
724-9440

This restaurant's namesake wouldn't be fooled for a minute by the brown-varnished plywood pseudo-Renaissance decoration, but it is easy to forgive in view of a more basic virtue—fresh white tablecloths bearing wine and water glasses polished to a high sparkle. The "complete dinner" doesn't include hor d'oeuvre, but you are not likely to miss them. The entrées give evidence that somebody in the kitchen likes his job. We enjoyed one special of the day, soft-shell crabs that could hardly have been improved on, and chicken à la mode, which was breast stuffed with ham and cheese, bathed in brown sauce, with string beans generously sprinkled with garlic, half a grilled tomato, and carrots. When things are not raucous at the bar (which has a jukebox) this is a pleasant, quiet spot.

Cocktails, wines and beer.

At lunch, à la carte dishes cost from about $2 to $5.50. Table d'hôte dinners cost from about $7.00 to $11.50. Brunch is from $2.50 to $5.50.

Open 7 days a week from 11:00 a.m. until 11:30 p.m. Sunday brunch is from noon until 4:00 p.m.

Reservations recommended for dinner.

AE   DC   MC

★★ LES MAREYEURS

998 Madison Avenue (between 77th and 78th Streets)
628-3333

When Les Mareyeurs opened in February, 1975, we gave it three stars on the basis of some absolutely first-rate dishes and a break regarding the service because the restaurant was still in its shakedown period. However, there have been enough complaints about hoity-toity captains to make us feel safer in cutting the stars down to two. But the restaurant gets top marks for its general appearance, with aquariums used as room dividers between the bar and restaurant areas and a quietly elegant decorative scheme in general.

It's a fish restaurant but very French—none of that chummy, elbow-to-elbow beachside air that so many fish restaurants cultivate.

Sampling eight different entrées, we found that those prepared with sauces were far and away the best; others somehow seemed dried out. As a matter of fact, this is a difficult restaurant to evaluate. It has a four-star look, serves some four-star dishes, fails badly on others, and has variable service. I'd say give it a try and hope for the best. Its best is very good indeed.

Cocktails, wines and beer.

All dishes are à la carte, with main courses at midday

beginning from about $4.75; in the evening, from about $7.50.

Open Monday through Saturday, except summer, from noon until 10:00 p.m.

Closed Sunday and all major holidays. Closed Monday and Saturday from Memorial to Labor Day.

Reservations recommended at dinner.

In the fall, there is a pianist during dinner.

AE

★★ LES PLEIADES
20 East 76th Street   535-7230-1

Les Pleiades boasts a star cluster of art dealers and museum directors for whom it is the neighborhood beanery at lunch time. At dinner the clientele runs more to inhabitants of the apartment houses on Fifth and Park Avenues. For reasons we have never been able to figure out after numerous anonymous visits at both times of day, the lunch trade gets a much better shake, both as to service and food. It is difficult to forget and forgive a dinner party for eight when we were served a gray substance so devoid of flavor that it was only by deduction that we identified it as veal, while we were all but showered in bottle after bottle of a Burgundy that must have cost our hostess a fortune. The glasses were not only filled to the brim on the first go-round but were kept that way throughout the meal, with a few dollars' worth spilled on the tablecloth during pouring. It was a rushed night when the place was crowded preceding an important auction at the nearby Parke-Bernet Galleries, but if that is an explanation, it isn't an excuse.

But at lunch we have been beautifully served in a room where the gloss has sufficiently faded from the décor to give a comfortable air to an interior that is still stylish. Shrimp and fish dishes are excellent at Les

Pleiades. Maybe it's only a case of consistently bad luck at dinner and consistently good luck at lunch. Odd, though.

Cocktails, wines and beer.

All dishes are à la carte, with main courses at midday from about $4.75 to $5.50; in the evening, from about $7.50 to $8.00.

Open Monday through Saturday from noon until 11:00 p.m. Open Sunday for parties.

Closed Sunday, except for parties and banquets. Also closed Labor Day and the month of August.

Reservations recommended.

AE MC

★ LE STEAK

1089 Second Avenue (near 57th Street)   421-9072

There's just one entrée here, a good steak in a mustard and tarragon sauce. With it comes a pile of french fries that are—or used to be—the best in the city, and a salad, then a choice among desserts. A few years ago Le Steak was one of our four or five favorite restaurants and we would have given it three stars without hesitation, but well enough hasn't been left alone. It is still an attractive little restaurant but the cozy air, with waitresses in approximations of provincial French dress, has been sacrificed in a generally sleek remodeling.

However, still good.

Cocktails, wines and beer.

Open for dinner only with a prix fixe at $9.95.

Open 7 days a week, from 5:30 to 11:00 p.m.

Closed Christmas, New Year's Day, Easter, Labor Day and Thanksgiving.

Reservations recommended.

AE DC

★★ L'ESTEREL

1063 First Avenue (at 58th Street)   PL 9-2630

L'Estérel is a welcome newcomer among promising French restaurants. Marguerite, the chef, and Rita, the manager out front, took over the quarters of the defunct La Croisette, brightened them up, whipped a new staff into an efficient corps, and started all over again in the kitchen. Duckling with olives, which has a very tasty sauce, seems to be establishing itself as the favorite dish here. It is ours, but we have liked everything else we have tried so far.

Cocktails, wines and beer.

A la carte dishes at lunch are from $1.75 and up; table d'hôte lunches are from $6.50 and up. At dinner, main courses are from $7.75 and up.

Open Monday through Thursday from noon until 10:30 p.m.; Friday and Saturday until 11:00 p.m.

Closed Sunday and all major holidays, except Easter.

Reservations recommended.

Party and banquet facilities available for up to 50 guests.

AE BA MC

★ LE VEAU D'OR

129 East 60th Street   TE 8-8133

Le Veau d'Or seems to be the favorite French restaurant of about half the restaurant-going public in New York, and to suggest that it has a flaw is to lose friends. However, our opinion that it is overcrowded and drastically overrated is not going to influence enough people to damage its thriving business, and its popularity is indeed deserved on the basis of its dependability. If it doesn't rise to any special heights, it never lets you down.

Cocktails, wines and beer.

All dishes are table d'hôte, with midday prices from about

$6.10 to $9.10; in the evening, from about $9.30 to $16.00.

Open Monday through Saturday from noon until 10:00 p.m.

Closed Sunday, the last 3 weeks of August through Labor Day, and all major holidays.

Reservations accepted.

No credit cards.

★ LUCHOW'S

110 East 14th Street   477-4860

Lüchow's is an institution, the great grand-daddy of German restaurants in New York. Neither the food nor the service is marked by much finesse, but the question from Lüchow fans, confronted by their hearty platters, would be, "With all this, who wants finesse?" It's a convivial place, with a genuine turn-of-the-century atmosphere where all diners are joined in their special kind of gustatory brotherhood.

Cocktails, wines and beer.

At lunch, table d'hôte costs from about $3.95 to $5.95; à la carte entrées from about $4.95 to $11.95. The table d'hôte dinner costs from about $8.95 to $12.95, with the à la carte menu priced from about $4.95 to $11.95.

Open 7 days a week from 11:00 a.m. until 9:30 p.m.

Reservations recommended and required at Christmas time.

Oompah band and Viennese strings play nitely.

AE   BA   CD   DC   MC

★★★ LUTECE

249 East 50th Street   PL 2-2225

Lutèce (the ancient name for Paris, and still given to an old quarter of the Ile de la Cité) is many gourmets' choice for New York's best French restaurant. It is certainly our choice as the prettiest, from match boxes and menu covers to wall coverings and curtains. With its enchanting glass-roofed garden at the rear of the first floor and its elegant high-ceilinged rooms on the second, it is the only two-floor restaurant we can think of where one location isn't thought of as second-best to the other.

In or out of France, a restaurant just doesn't get any more French, in either atmosphere or cuisine, than Lutèce. In this case it means a particularly strong emphasis on sauces, sauces, sauces. And more sauces. The service is usually deft but, surprisingly, there is sometimes a most inelegant clatter of copper pans and china during operations at the serving tables, and the dishes are stacked up when being removed from your table, hash-house fashion—a disharmonious note in a restaurant where everything else is conducive to a feeling that you are being beautifully taken care of under the most leisurely circumstances. Even so, the prospect of dinner at Lutèce is enough to inspire an anticipatory glow forty-eight hours in advance.

Cocktails, wines and beer.

Table d'hôte lunch is about $13.75. A la carte entrées at dinner cost from about $26 to $28.00.

Open from Monday through Friday from noon until 9:45 p.m.; Saturday from 5:45 p.m. to 9:45 p.m.

Closed for lunch on Saturdays, all day Sunday and all major holidays.

Reservations required.

AE

★ MALAGA
406 East 73rd Street   737-7659

Malaga is a simple—almost a rough—little
Spanish restaurant as to décor and we have found it
very uneven in the kitchen, the same dish coming out
beautifully one night and sadly the next. Its location
and lack of pretension have made it a popular neighborhood restaurant and you will probably come off
best by asking the waiter what's good tonight and
following his advice, although there is an extensive
menu listing 20 seafood entrées and 15 meats. The atmosphere is happy, with couples sitting around drinking sangría.

Cocktails, wines and beer.

*All dishes are à la carte, with main courses at midday from
about $3.25 to $4.95; in the evening, from about $4.25 to $7.25.*

*Open 7 days a week from noon until midnight; Friday and
Saturday until 1:00 a.m.*

Reservations accepted.

AE   BA   DC   MC

★ MAMA LAURA
230 East 58th Street   MU 8-6888

The address is fashionable but the kitchen is as
homey as the name. Enjoy.

Cocktails, wines and beer.

*At lunch, à la carte dishes cost from about $3.75 to $6.00.
There is a prix fixe dinner at $11.50, with à la carte entrées
from $5.25 to $9.50.*

Open 7 days a week from noon until 11:30 p.m.

*Closed July 4th, Labor Day, Christmas and Memorial
Day.*

Reservations recommended.

All major credit cards.

176

★★★ MANDARIN HOUSE
133 West 13th Street   WA *9-0551*

Many other friends as devoted as we were be-
moan the demise of Mandarin East, which was once,
but alas is no longer, just north of 57th Street on Second Avenue. But Mandarin House, its parent downtown, not only survives but is rejuvenated, having
inherited Mandarin East's kitchen staff and, hence, its
third star.

Our favorite dish at Mandarin East was spicy bean
curd home-style. It is now available at Mandarin
House along with the rest of a menu that includes
delectable versions of such general favorites as moo
shu pork.

Mandarin House has a garden that is available to
fairly large parties in fall and winter for a kind of
cook-out called Mongolian barbecue, where food is
prepared on the spot on an outdoor Chinese stove,
with an array of Chinese sauces as accompaniment. This kind of party of course has to be arranged in advance with Emily Kwoh, the proprietor.

Cocktails, wines and beer.

*Complete lunches cost from about $2.00 to $3.00; table
d'hôte dinners are from about $5.00 to $7.00.*

Open 7 days a week from noon until 10:00 p.m.

Reservations accepted.

AE CB DC MC

★ MANEEYA THAI
926 Eighth Avenue (between 54th and 55th Streets)
586-9838

The authenticity of the food at Maneeya Thai
is vouched for by the people you'll find eating there—
Thai and Vietnamese residents of the neighborhood.

It is a simple place, family-run. Among dishes that you should like are chicken ginger (small pieces of chicken lightly sautéed with herbs and served in a pretty ring of crisp Chinese parsley) and cha kho, a whole fish simmered in a sauce of various herbs to give it a wonderfully crisp browned skin over the most delicate white flesh. This is an inexpensive restaurant for New York and you eat well.

No liquor; bring your own wine.

Lunch is from $3.25 and up; dinner dishes are from $5.95 and up.

Open 7 days a week, except for Monday lunch.

Open Tuesday through Sunday from 11:45 a.m. until midnight; Monday from 5:00 p.m. until midnight.

Closed for Monday lunch.

Reservations recommended.

AE

★★ MANNY WOLF'S CHOP HOUSE

Third Avenue (at 49th Street)   *355-5030*

Manny's—to get on a first name basis right away—has been around forever, which goes to prove that if people like your food, they don't mind what they have to go through to get it. Manny's clientele, as a matter of fact, seems to think of the noise and the crowding as a kind of palatable garnish to charcoal broiled chateaubriand steaks and chicken with matzoh balls. An institution.

Cocktails, wines and beer.

All dishes are à la carte, with main courses at midday from about $4.45 to $10.95; in the evening, from about $6.95 to $11.75.

Open 7 days a week from 11:30 a.m. until 11:30 p.m.

Reservations recommended.

AE   CB   DC   MC

★★ MARCHI'S

251 East 31st Street (near Second Avenue)   *679-2494*

Marchi's opened in, as we remember, one room in 1930, and since then has grown bigger and bigger and yet bigger. There's no menu; you go in and have dinner as it comes that night, and it goes on and on, amazingly. The cuisine is North Italian at a high level, and in spite of the restaurant's size it still generates the atmosphere of a family celebration.

Cocktails, wines and beer.

Open for dinner only with prix fixe dinner at $9.75.

Open from Monday through Friday from 5:15 p.m. until 10:15 p.m.; Saturday until 11:15 p.m.

Closed Sunday.

Reservations recommended.

Jackets required. No blue jeans or sneakers.

AE

★★★ MARIO'S VILLA d'ESTE

58 East 56th Street   PL 9-4025-6

Warning: Our rating of three stars for Mario's Villa d'Este drew yawps of protest from numerous gastronomes familiar with the place, and we admit that it has faults that we have forgiven because we find it a happy place to dine. What with red and gold everywhere, and mirrors and tinted photomurals (of the gardens of the real Villa d'Este) and bits of ornamental iron work and pots of convincing but artificial pink roses, plus red and green tinted lights here and there, it sounds like too much, but the room has a kind of overdecorated coziness with a pretty fountain as its centerpiece that we like.

All right, so the waiter didn't ask how we wanted the lamb chops and we'd have liked them pinker than they came. All right, so the room can get noisy if

179

there's a table or two of inconsiderate diners (hardly the restaurant's fault). And we have felt a little pushed at lunch when we arrived late, the service, normally efficient, becoming a little too fast. And the vegetables leave a lot to be desired.

It's a sheer case of favoritism, probably. But when you feel happy somewhere—why not?

Favorite dishes include, for openers, avocado vinaigrette, half an avocado filled with a crisp, tangy combination of chopped vegetables, cannelloni (which is first-rate and can also be had as an entrée), and the combination plate of hot hors d'oeuvre.

Among entrées, we've been happy with breast of capon Villa d'Este, which is prepared with prosciutto, cheese, and wine sauce, and another chicken dish, rollatini à la Mario, prepared with prosciutto, herbs, and spinach with mushroom sauce. Three stars? For us, yes.

Cocktails, wines and beer.

The prix fixe luncheon is about $7.00. Prix fixe dinners cost from about $9.50 to $12.50, with an à la carte menu starting at $5.00.

Open 7 days a week from noon until 11:00 p.m.

Closed Christmas.

Reservations recommended.

AE   BA   CB   DC   MC

★★★★ **MAXWELL'S PLUM**
64th Street and First Avenue   628-2100

We can hear it now: "Four stars for Maxwell's Plum? Are you out of your mind?" Four stars, absolutely. Without any question, this is New York's most spectacular restaurant, and if its theatrical décor has an equal anywhere else, we haven't run across it. The modest-looking glassed-in sidewalk terrace as seen from the street doesn't hint at the art nouveau palace behind it, where an elaborate bar and café lead to a raised dining room where the service and atmosphere are a bit more elegant. Everywhere, genuine turn-of-the-century works of art and curiosa have been combined with reproductions and inventions in the same spirit, including a ceiling reconstructed from Tiffany glass and illuminated from behind.

This obviously isn't your standard four-star restaurant with an air of conventional elegance and leisurely dining. People line up behind ropes waiting for places. The bar is crowded with everything from swinging singles to visiting school teachers, the café tables are filled with the motliest of crews ("motley" at Maxwell's Plum is so all-inclusive a term that Brooks Brothers button-down types are right in there with everybody else) and the dining room proper—more or less proper—accommodates celebrities, Beautiful People, college kids, and you name it. Preferential treatment of big names and big spenders is held to a minimum.

Four stars? You bet. The food is excellent to superb, and the kitchen's ability to keep the dishes coming without loss of quality to so many tables means that the whole place is a miracle of organization.

You haven't seen New York until you've at least had a drink at Maxwell's Plum.

Cocktails, wines and beer.

All dishes are à la carte, with main courses at midday from about $2.95 to $7.50. The brunch and after-theatre menu is the same. The à la carte items at dinner cost from about $2.95 to $9.85.

*Open 7 days a week from noon until midnight. The café
is open until 1:30 a.m.*

Reservations recommended.

All major credit cards.

★★ MESON BOTIN

145 West 58th Street   265-4567

This is a large restaurant ambitiously decorated
in hybrid approximations of Spanish medieval and
Renaissance style, with full suits of armor (the genuine article) among the ornaments. It's all very
baronial, and you are likely to find your fellow diners
at the next tables speaking Spanish, as if getting into
the act.

Trencherman's portions are not unusual in Spanish
restaurants (here and in Spain) but they seemed
unusually large to us at Meson Botin. An order of
pimiento à la Riojana (stuffed sweet red peppers in
batter) brought three enormous peppers of which we
could eat only one, half another, and mangle the third.
Pepitoria de gallina (large pieces of chicken in a sauce
of eggs and saffron) is one of the best dishes here. But
there are many, including such very Spanish specialties as baby octopus in oil and tripe Madrid style. And,
of course paella and gazpacho among the more familiar items.

Cocktails, wines and beer.

*All dishes are à la carte, with main courses at midday from
about $3.40 to $6.75; in the evening, from about $4.50 to $9.50.*

Open 7 days a week from noon until 11:00 p.m.

Closed all major holidays.

Reservations recommended.

AE   CB   DC

★★ MEXICAN GARDENS
137 Waverly Place   243-9878

Don't expect a garden at Mexican Gardens. It's a half-basement, one of those Greenwich Village interiors with several decades of amateur enamel paint jobs overlaid on the woodwork, with all the scabs and scars of time embedded therein. What you can expect, though, is superior this-side-of-the-border Mexican food cheerfully served in generous portions. We have found that the best bet here has been flautas (king-size tacos with meat) and, as an appetizer, nachos. These are a standard item (tostada chips, a thin layer of bean paste, a piece of cheese, grilled and topped with a slice of hot pepper) but the Mexican Gardens' are the best in New York.

No style, but a good place.

Cocktails, wines and beer.

At lunch, à la carte dishes cost from about $1.90 to $4.60. The dinner menu costs from about $3.95 and includes soup, rice and beans and dessert.

Open 7 days a week. Open Sunday through Thursday from noon until 1:00 a.m. (except Tuesday for lunch, see below). Open Friday and Saturday to 2:00 a.m.

Closed Tuesday for lunch. Also closed Thanksgiving, Christmas and New Year's Day.

No reservations.

No credit cards.

★★ MILLER'S
Woolworth Building, 233 Broadway   CO 7-3156

Miller's, probably the best restaurant in the City Hall area, has something special that no other restaurant in the world can boast—the lobby of the Woolworth Building, which you have to walk through

183

to reach the stairs leading down to the basement. It is the most beautiful lobby of any New York office building and in addition has reached the status of historical monument and period piece.

The restaurant in a simpler way is in style with the lobby, a neo-Gothic low-vaulted room that also suggests pre-war German rathskellers, especially Dresden's. The menu indicates that the city fathers and Wall Street brokers who eat here favor good, simple, hearty food in he-man portions. We sampled roast beef and grilled striped bass ("Hand-painted stripes," the waiter said. He alone laughed.) and decided that the men who determine the fate of our city must be honest, sturdy fellows with fantastic digestive systems. Unless they go back to the office from Miller's and collapse for the afternoon. Possible.

Cocktails, wines and beer.

A la carte entrées at lunch begin at about $7.75. Table d'hôte dinners start from about $8.75.

Open Monday through Friday from 11:30 a.m. until last order at 8:00 p.m.

Closed Saturday, Sunday and all major holidays.

No reservations.

Private dining room, seating up to 60 guests, is available.

AE   MC

★★ MR. LEE'S

337 Third Avenue (at 25th Street)   MU 9-6373

The corner of Third Avenue and 25th Street isn't exactly tucked away in a quiet spot, but Mr. Lee's, at that address, qualifies as a little out-of-the-way restaurant. Neither uptown nor downtown, it combines the intimacy and informality that you expect in the Village with aspirations to haute cuisine that would do credit to plush spots in the 50's. The double standard doesn't always dovetail, but the misses are easy to excuse in view of the good nature that permeates the place.

The tables are attractively set up, with a still life of breads, an apple and cheese arranged on a wooden platter ready for you when you sit down, along with candles and some modest flowers. The diners have the air of habitués enjoying one another's company in a favorite hideaway, and you could do a lot worse than to join them for an evening.

It isn't exactly inexpensive, but the kitchen really cares about what it serves. Along with a generally French cuisine you will find such oddities as a cold apricot, orange, and yogurt soup (it would have done as well for dessert), prettily served on its tray of ice.

Wines and beer.

All dishes are à la carte, with main courses at midday from about $2.95 to $9.50; in the evening, from about $7.25 to $12.50.

Open Monday through Saturday from noon until 11:00 p.m.

Closed Sunday and all major holidays.

Reservations accepted.

All major credit cards.

★★ MONK'S INN, THE
35 West 64th Street   *874-2710*

Immediate proximity to Lincoln Center is the Monk's Inn's most conspicuous virtue, but it can also more than hold its own independently as a restaurant. Its hallmarks are a staggering collection of cheeses, and waiters scurrying around in monk's garb. You half expect them to recite the menu in plainsong, but they come through in ordinary Manhattanese, offer-

185

ing you fondues, rarebits, omelets, and Swiss and Alsatian fare such as kraut, bratwurst and pigs' knuckles. The scene is laid with beams, paneling, stained-glass windows, dripping candles, and all those other storybook things.

Cocktails, wines and beer.

All dishes are à la carte, with main courses at midday from about $4 to $8.00; in the evening, from about $5 to $10.00.

Open 7 days a week from noon until 12:30 a.m.

Reservations recommended.

AE   BA   CB   DC   MC

★ **MON PARIS**

111 East 29th Street   MU *4-9152*

This is a very popular restaurant—understandably, since it can be depended on to turn out bourgeois French cooking at a much better than average level, and to serve it to you cheerfully. We miss a certain grace in the general atmosphere and an individual note in the kitchen that make the difference between a very good restaurant and a good workaday performance, but the consistency of the performance is admirable.

Cocktails, wines and beer.

A la carte entrées at lunch cost about $2.25 to $4.50. Table d'hôte dinners are from about $6.75 to $12.50.

Open Monday through Saturday from noon until 10:30 p.m.

Closed Sunday and all major holidays. Also closed July and August until Labor Day.

Reservations recommended at dinner.

AE

★★ MONTE CARMELA

1643 First Avenue (near 85th Street)   628-6266

From the window of a taxi en route to another restaurant we noticed Monte Carmela's good Italian name and the string of lights across its façade and jotted it down for a visit. It turns out to be as good as its wrapping—a second-generation family restaurant that recently moved to this Yorkville address from farther uptown. You can depend on beautiful pastas here; other dishes are variable, but prices, including wines, are kept low enough to atone for a few defects.

Cocktails, wines and beer.

Open for dinner only with à la carte items costing from about $3.95 to $7.75.

Open Wednesday through Monday. Open Sunday, Monday, Wednesday and Thursday from 4:00 p.m. until 11:00 p.m.; Friday and Saturday open until midnight.

Closed Tuesday, Thanksgiving and Christmas.

No reservations.

No credit cards.

★ MOSHE PEKING

40 West 37th Street   594-6500

Moshe Peking is the more glamorous of two kosher-Chinese restaurants in New York, but the food in neither as good nor as Chinese as at its totally unglamorous rival, Bernstein-on-Essex Street (which see, for some comments on ways and means of reconciling Chinese cuisine with kosher dietary laws). But it is very popular in the garment district and other areas within easy taxi distance for lunch, and has, indeed, a very nicely got-up interior with the cheerfulest service in the world.

A lot of the dishes are only semi-Chinese to begin with and require no modifications, such as lemon chicken, which comes simply as boned chicken breasts breaded with a little lemon squeezed over. Shellfish being prohibited by Jewish dietary laws, we were interested in how approximations would be made. The very name "pho-nee shrimp"—(get it?)—should have warned us, but we fell for it and hence are in a position to tell you to avoid at all costs these "cubes of tender fish in an authentically flavored sauce with Chinese vegetables and subtle seasonings," which were hardly edible.

Steak dishes were good, however, and in spite of everything we rather enjoyed Moshe Peking for the gaiety with which it went about its job.

Cocktails, wines and beer.

Complete luncheons are from about $4.95 to $7.50; à la carte dishes are from $6.50 to $10.00. Complete dinners are from about $13.90 to $41.70, which serve 2, 3, 4, 5 or 6 guests.

Open Monday through Friday evening in the summer. Sunday through Thursday from noon until 10:00 p.m.; Friday from noon until 2:00 p.m. In the winter, same, except Saturday open from 10:00 p.m. until 1:00 a.m. Closed all day Saturday and Saturday evenings. Also closed all Jewish holidays.

Reservations recommended.

AE   DC   MC

★★★ NANNI

146 East 46th Street   697-4161 and 687-9534

Whether or not this restaurant—usually called Nanni's, since the chef owns it—serves the best Italian food in New York depends on who's talking, but the place is so good that it has to be the best of something, perhaps the best Italian restaurant of its size. It's a small place, with a lot of style when you start examining details, from the nicely designed matchpacks to the waiters' uniforms. The little fellow running around in a plain white kitchen apron is Nanni himself. Service is excellent, diners are bright and happy looking, and the food for a typical dinner for two goes like this, by our choice:

Divided order of clams arreganato, excellent.

Divided order of linguine al pesto (when in season), superb.

Day's special, suggested by the waiter, a chicken breast flattened out, lightly breaded, sautéed with wine and mushroom sauce. First-rate.

Saltimbocca for the second person's entrée, veal scaloppini topped with prosciutto and cheese and sauced up. Good.

Salad, on the house. Lettuce, arugula, and tomatoes.

With all this, you're likely to have to pass up desserts. Excellent espressos, with plenty of refills included in the price, are a good wind-up.

Cocktails, wines and beer.

All dishes are à la carte, with main courses at midday from about $3.75 to $7.50; in the evening, from about $4.25 to $10.00.

Open Monday through Saturday from noon until 10:30 p.m.

Closed Sunday and all major holidays.

Reservations required.

AE   BA   DC   MC

★★ NICOLA PAONE

207 East 34th Street   889-3239

Nicola Paone is not to be confused under any circumstances with Nicola, a new uptown restaurant that has been omitted from this guide because of consistent rudeness to anonymous customers and refusal to honor reservations. Nicola Paone has been around for a long time and has a large and loyal following but doesn't play favorites. If you are not put off by specialties called "Nightgown" and "Boom Boom," which are in fact good variations on standard dishes with veal or chicken, ham, and cheese, you will find the menu classically Italian. The best dish we have had here is plain broiled chicken with garlic, which is far from being an elementary test of an Italian kitchen. Service is excellent, although prices are on the high side.

Cocktails, wines and beer.

All dishes are à la carte, with main courses at midday from about $7 to $11; in the evening, from about $9 to $14.00.

Open Monday through Saturday from noon until 9:00 p.m.

Closed Sunday, all major holidays and the last two weeks of August.

Reservations accepted.

Jacket and tie required.

AE   DC

★★   NIPPON
145 East 52nd Street   758-0226

Choosing among New York's numerous Japanese restaurants is difficult. A good solution is to try them all. Nippon strikes a happy balance between the slick semi-Westernized restaurants similar to the big ones in Tokyo that cater as much to tourists as to the Japanese, and the purely Japanese ones where you can even encounter language difficulties with the waitresses.

Nippon is operated efficiently and with graciousness. Having eaten there both as the guest of visiting Japanese journalists and as an anonymous drop-in, we can vouch for the consistent courtesy and good service. If you are familiar with Japanese food you'll have no trouble. If you aren't, let's suggest sunomono (crabmeat salad served with vinegar sauce), suimono (a tuna-and-seaweed-flavored soup), shabu-shabu (its name is supposed to imitate the sound made by boiling bouillon into which you dunk thin slices of beef or pork with vegetables for cooking at the table) and of course tempura, probably the favorite Japanese dish with Americans, which is assorted seafood and vegetables deep fried in a light batter. Or go on from there with the help of the menu or your waiter.

Nippon has attractive tatami rooms, straw-matted alcoves where you sit on the floor at a low table. But better arrange for these in advance. They are usually spoken for by Japanese.

Cocktails, wines and beer.

Complete luncheons are priced from about $3.50 to $6.80, with à la carte items beginning at $2.50 and up. Complete dinner is $8.50 and up, with à la carte entrées starting at $2.50.

Open Monday through Saturday, excluding Saturday lunch. Open Monday through Thursday from noon until 10:00 p.m.; Friday and Saturday until 10:30 p.m.

Closed Sunday. Also closed for Saturday dinner and dinner on all major holidays.

Reservations recommended.

AE CB DC

★★ NODELDINI'S

1311 Madison Avenue (at 93rd Street)   *369-5677 and 722-9489*

You may leave Nodeldini's bruised and deafened but you will also leave well fed on beautifully fresh fish. On a busy night—and they all seem to be busy—this is a medium-sized madhouse. On one occasion our waiter, who could have qualified as an Olympic gymnast solely on his demonstration of agility in reaching across a table for four in order to serve ours for two, said "Desperation—sheer desperation," when we asked him how he stood the racket and the crush.

But Nodeldini's is good enough so that it could double or triple its prices and fill its tables with a more sedate crowd. No matter how beset the waiter, no matter how tightly you may be squeezed into a corner, as soon as you are seated a bowl of salad greens is lofted to you with a tri-partite server that offers choices of dressing for tossing your own.

The legend is that somebody named Nodeldini goes out every day and catches his own fish for this restaurant. That can hardly be true, but the fish is pristine, simply prepared, and somehow gets to your table without delay in the perilous passage from the basement kitchen.

Cocktails, wines and beer.

At lunch, à la carte dishes cost from about $1.95 to $2.75. Dinner costs from about $3.95 to $5.50 and includes salad, garlic bread, vegetable and potato. Sunday brunch is $2.95 and includes 3 Bloody Marys.

Open 7 days a week from 11:30 a.m. until midnight. Brunch on Sunday is open from noon until 4:00 p.m.

No reservations.

No credit cards.

★ OGGI

1606 First Avenue (between 83rd and 84th Streets)
628-0383

Oggi goes in for large portions of Italian food prepared with skill if not finesse. There's no menu, and the waiter is likely to leave the list of available dishes incomplete when he recites them. A good idea if you like fish is to ask if there's something good in that line in the kitchen at the moment. Otherwise, it's ossobuco, veal Marsala, and other standards. There are also shrimp in white sauce, tender and tasty.

The clientele at Oggi, which regards itself as a neighborhood Yorkville restaurant, runs all the way from rolled-up shirtsleeves or T-shirts to three-piece suits and club ties, which speaks well for the food as a common denominator.

Cocktails, wines and beer.

Open for dinner only with à la carte items ranging from $3.75 to $7.25, which includes potato salad or spaghetti. Each day there is a different special which costs $5.75.

Open 7 days a week from 5:00 p.m. until midnight.

Closed Easter, July 4th, Labor Day, Thanksgiving, Christmas, New Year's Day and the last 2 weeks in July.

No reservations.

AE CB DC MC

★★ O LAR

27 West 72nd Street   799-7331

"O Lar" in Galician dialect means "homestead" or "hearthside," a name that is belied by the crisp and elegant décor of this ballroom-like restaurant with its sparkling chandeliers. The waiters, all of them young Spaniards, combine a real sense of style with efficiency.

With an occasional exception, such as shrimp ajillo, which has a hot garlic sauce with a peppery bite, the food at O Lar has the blandness so frequently characteristic of Spanish food. An unadventurous friend chose a plain broiled sirloin and found it excellent and, $8.75 at that time, reasonably priced.

Cocktails, wines and beer.

A la carte entrées at lunch cost from about $3 to $5. Complete dinners are priced from about $8.25 to $12.25, with à la carte items from about $5.50 to $9.75.

Open Monday through Thursday from 11:00 a.m. until midnight; Friday and Saturday until 1:00 a.m.

Closed Sunday.

Reservations recommended at dinner.

AE   DC   MC

★★ ONDE'S

945 Second Avenue (between 50th and 51st Streets)
751-9631

This is one of many New York places that change character between late afternoon and early evening, turning from a straight restaurant into a semi-supperclub with the addition of a featured performer. Since the performer does a great deal to set the character of the place, and since there are changes, we can vouch only for the food and the lunchtime character.

The atmosphere is one of rather plushy intimacy in rather close quarters. The cuisine is French-Italian, with the accent on Italian, and the dishes we have tried have been uniformly well prepared. A spinach salad, loaded with bacon and mushrooms, was especially good. Pastas have arrived al dente without special request, always a good sign, and eggplant Parmigiana was a little violent—the way we happen to like it.

The greeting is warm, service is good, and there is a cheerful spirit throughout.

Cocktails, wines and beer.

All dishes are à la carte, with main courses at midday from *about $4 to $6.25; in the evening, from about $6 to $9.25.*

Open Monday through Saturday from 11:30 a.m. until midnight.

Closed Sunday, 4th of July, Thanksgiving, Christmas and New Year's Day.

Reservations recommended.

Pianist every evening from 7:00 to midnight.

AE   BA   CB   MC

★★ ONE IF BY LAND, TWO IF BY SEA
17 Barrow Street   255-8649

This curiously named restaurant has become so popular that you can hardly get a table, is so crowded that you can hardly push through to your table after you get it, and is so noisy that once you get seated you can shout your most intimate secrets to your dinner partner without fear of being heard, much less overheard. We have had reports of rudeness from the waiters since last visiting the place, but the worst we could complain of was that they were so busy that their manner was somewhat abrupt when they finally got around to us.

The menu lists only six entrées, seven hors d'oeuvre, two salads, a soup du jour, and a daily special. As an opener, either the spinach, raw mushroom and bacon salad, or the marinated salmon with dill mustard is excellent, and enough for two. Beef Wellington is a big favorite here; I can't report that it is exceptional. Veal steak, very good if not exciting, is a large portion sautéed with an unobtrusive tomato sauce and garnished with artichokes and watercress.

The restaurant is entered by way of a large, exceptionally attractive bar area with sofas in front of a couple of chummy fireplaces. The large balcony tends to be less noisy than the main floor, but at either level the racket is deafening, what with loud voices of diners mingling with either the jukebox or a piano. Some people, of course, like all that. One If by Land, Two if By Sea, is, to say the very least, a convivial place.

Cocktails, wines and beer.

Open for dinner only with à la carte entrées from about $7.95 to $12.95.

Open 7 days a week, except July and August, from 6:00 p.m. until 11:00 p.m.

Closed Monday during July and August. Also closed July 4th, New Year's Day and Labor Day.

Reservations recommended.

AE   CB   DC   MC

★ **ORSINI'S**

41 West 56th Street   PL *7-1698*

In its sparkling elegance, Orsini's is equaled but hardly surpassed by any other restaurant in New York as a beautiful spot for dining. The trouble is that you are more likely to be seated at one of the tables near the bar or in the vestibule leading to the dining room where all you see is the beautiful people en route to their tables and the coattails of the waiters bearing them their food. This food is good, too, but we have taken a star from Orsini's here because you are more likely than not to be greeted with a kind of hauteur that seems to question your presence there. Too bad.

Cocktails, wines and beer.

All dishes are à la carte, with main courses at midday from about $6 to $8; in the evening, from about $8 to $12.75.

Open Monday through Saturday from noon until 1:00 a.m.

Closed Sunday, July 4th, Labor Day, Christmas and New Year's Day.

Reservations required at lunch; recommended at dinner.
AE   CB   DC   MC

★★★ OYSTER BAR AND RESTAURANT IN GRAND CENTRAL TERMINAL

42nd Street and Park Avenue   532-3888

Recently reopened after a closure for refurbishing, this 62-year-old fish and seafood restaurant seems to be keeping up once more to the standards that made it a New York favorite until a decline in the 1960's. There's always just plain great oyster stew at the bar, but there are also full fish and seafood dinners from a vast menu that lists everything, whether or not it is available that day. An institution reborn.

Cocktails, wines and beer.

At lunch and dinner, à la carte dishes cost from about $3.75 to $6.75.

Open Monday through Friday from 11:30 until 10:30 p.m. Reservations accepted.

AE   BA   CB   DC   MC

$$$$ PALACE, THE

420 East 59th Street (between First Avenue and Sutton Place)   355-5152

With a $50 prix fixe, 8 percent New York tax, and 23 percent obligatory service charge, it costs you $65.50 just to sit down at The Palace and you've still got your drinks and wine (up to $400 a bottle) to pay for. Omitting the drinks and choosing a moderately priced wine on our only visit, two of us got out for $196.50, but we don't know of anyone else who has broken a hundred per person.

The idea is that you can choose anything you want on the seven-course menu without the supplementary charges for special items (including caviar) that are usual in other fancy prix fixe restaurants where, by making a little effort, you could rack up a comparable check.

If we were making another visit to The Palace we would order from the "sur commande" menu, which means choosing special dishes up to 48 hours in advance. The kitchen can turn out marvelous food and would no doubt rise to the challenge. But if you feel you can't wait to eat in New York's (perhaps the world's?) most expensive restaurant, you will have a wide variety of temptations on the regular menu. Count on three hours for the meal; it took us from eight in the evening until after midnight.

Because of the impossibility of averaging quality and price in this instance, we have omitted a star rating and applied one about which there is no question.

Cocktails, wines and beer.

Open for dinner only with a prix fixe at $50.00 (includes caviar, if desired).

Open from Monday through Saturday from 6:15 to 10:30 p.m.

Closed Sunday.

AE   BA   DC   MC

★★ PALM and PALM TOO
837 and 840 Second Avenue (near 45th Street)   MU 2-9515
and 683-7630

These twin restaurants across the street from one another begin bursting at the seams about eight o'clock, and after you finish dinner at either your own seams may not be in too good condition. Whether you have lobster, steak, filet, lamb chops, or roast beef—which is the menu—you are going to have to be a trencherman of great prowess to clear your plate.

Even so, you are making a mistake if you don't take a side order of cottage fried potatoes, a specialty that is a cross between potato chips and pommes soufflées. One order will do nicely for two. Or three.

The atmosphere is heavily in the tradition of sawdust floors and boisterous living. The steaks are marvelous—charred black on the outside and whatever you asked for on the inside, from bloody to pink to brown. Too late, I asked the waiter if they ever divided a steak between two diners, and he said, "We'll do anything." If not, there's always the doggie bag.

Cocktails, wines and beer.

All dishes are à la carte, with main courses at both lunch and dinner costing from about $7 to $21.00.

Open Monday through Saturday from noon until 11:45 p.m.

Closed Sunday, the first 2 weeks in July, Thanksgiving, Christmas and New Year's Day.

Reservations required at lunch.

All major credit cards.

★★ PANCHO VILLA'S

1501 Second Avenue (at 78th Street)　　*650-1455*

This Mexican (naturally) restaurant can be recommended to anyone fond of overeating on a modest budget. In the course of our visits we have been able to try nearly everything on the menu except the combination plates of enchiladas, tostadas, tamales, and burritos, taking it for granted that these would follow suit if we found the slightly more elaborate dishes satisfactory. They were.

We found one beautiful surprise among the appetizers—ceviche (marinated raw fish), which seldom comes off as well as it should this side of the Rio Grande. The marinade was lemon, onions, and a green leaf, probably cilantro, as it should have been.

Ingredients at Pancho Villa's are of high quality, which you can't usually depend on in Mexican restaurants. There's a very good homemade hot pepper sauce on the table for addition to your dishes if you like them very hot. (We do.)

Service is excellent, the atmosphere is genuinely friendly and festive, and there's a draft down the center of the room every time the front door opens, so sit somewhere else if it's chilly weather. There are musicians on some nights, but this is variable, and if you are interested in hitting such a night, better phone.

Cocktails, wines and beer.

At lunch, à la carte dishes cost from about $3.25 and up; at dinner the à la carte items cost from about $3.95 and up.

Open 7 days a week. Open Sunday through Thursday from noon until midnight; on Friday and Saturday until 1:00 a.m.

Closed Thanksgiving and Christmas.

Reservations recommended.

No credit cards.

★★ PANTHEON
689 Eighth Avenue (between 43rd and 44th Streets)
JU 6-9672

Year in, year out, this unpretentious and immaculate little Greek restaurant maintains its steady level of good food and good service. If we were sure what Greek home cooking is like, we might say that the Pantheon serves it. Moussaka, spinach and cheese pie, lemon soup, bean soup, stewed chicken—usual dishes, full of flavor and devoid of frills, reasonably priced. The good American bar also has Greek wines. Convenient to the theatres.

Cocktails, wines and beer.

All dishes are à la carte and cost from about $3.75 to $5.50 at both lunch and dinner.

Open Monday through Saturday from 11:30 a.m. until 11:00 p.m.

Closed Sunday.

No reservations.

No credit cards.

★ PARADISE RESTAURANT

347 West 41st Street LO 3-2581

The name promises a little too much, but this is a good Greek restaurant with amazingly low prices—which, these days, may be paradise enow. Fairly large and quite simple, the restaurant clears an area for Greek music and dancing on occasion. Ask when.

Cocktails, wines and beer.

There is a special luncheon costing $2.45, which includes soup, salad and coffee. The à la carte menu at dinner is priced from about $2.50 to $5.00. Brunch items cost from $1.50 to $2.50.

Open 7 days a week from 11:00 a.m. to 1:00 a.m.

Reservations recommended.

AE BA

★★★★ PARIOLI ROMANISSIMO

1466 First Avenue (between 76th and 77th Streets) 288-2391

This Roman-Italian restaurant gets up to three stars on the usual terms and rises to a nice, bright fourth on several exceptional scores. Excellent in the first place, the majority of the entrées are also unique to the house as variations on classical recipes. The place has real style without ostentation and is small enough (something like 11 tables) so that Rubrio Rossi, who created the restaurant, can get around to your table to answer questions about the menu and give advice if you want it. The single drawback is that the small room can get noisy.

If you want our advice as well as Mr. Rossi's, we can tell you that the veal scaloppini capriccio, sautéed with prosciutto and Fontina cheese in Marsala and touched off with a bit of mushroom, a dash of paprika, a strip of pimento, and a panache of parsley, is hard to beat. But it has a close rival in pescatora alla Veneziana, which includes calamari (freshly cooked), mussels, clams, shrimp, and whatever fish of the day is in the kitchen, with white wine sauce, onions, and saffron, plus just a touch of tomato instead of the heavy sauce that often ruins such a dish in Italian restaurants. The pastas are great, with a rich but marvelously light cannelloni. In the 10 years or so since we've known this restaurant (formerly much simpler than it is now) we've never heard any but enthusiastic reports.

Cocktails and wines.

Open for dinner only, with the à la carte dishes priced from about $7.00 to $11.00.

Open Monday through Saturday from 6:00 p.m. to 11:00 p.m.

Closed Sunday, the month of July and all major holidays.

Reservations required.

AE DC

★★ PARIS BISTRO
48 Barrow Street   989-5460

Paris Bistro cultivates an ambiance that is informal but not rakish and sets as its standard "good food moderately priced with a limited menu to choose from." They live up to that pretty well. As usual in this type of restaurant, your best bet is likely to be the plat du jour, since the single chef in the small kitchen will have settled on something especially good in the market at the moment and will be all set and ready to go with it.

However, let's mention that the chicken with apples and fruit sauce, on the regular menu, is exceptional. All portions are generous and accompanied by vegetables that, apparently, the chef makes a fetish of not overcooking. We have had zucchini still crisp—really only half cooked, or less, which is fine by us.

Cocktails, wines and beer.

Open for dinner only with the à la carte menu ranging from $4.95 to $9.50.

Open 7 days a week from 6:00 p.m. until 11:45 p.m.

Closed Christmas.

Reservations recommended.

AE   BA   DC   MC

★★★ PEARL'S CHINESE RESTAURANT
38 West 48th Street   586-1060

Pearl's is the empress of New York Chinese restaurants. Now in its third incarnation after a modest beginning, it is sleekly installed in quarters that have the one disadvantage of bouncing the slightest sound off the walls in every direction. But Pearl's fans (count us in) are never deterred by the threat of deafness as part payment for the assurance of gustatory delight.

We prefer to go to Pearl's in a party of four to six people in order to share a number of dishes—six to eight—and usually leave it up to Pearl herself to make the choices, stipulating a greater or lesser percentage of spicy items according to the tastes of the particular group. Always for out-of-towners, however, we include the lemon chicken that has become Pearl's hallmark. In small pieces it is easily divided around the table. Sometimes we order doubles.

Pearl's cuisine is basically Cantonese with some Western modifications that amount to refinements rather than concessions to American taste. Unless you are extremely lucky you won't get in for dinner without a reservation 24 hours in advance. Pearl's is within reach of the Broadway theatres, but if you take advantage of this, be sure to go early enough to allow time to savor the food and walk the unexpectedly long blocks to the theatre district proper.

Cocktails, wines and beer.

All dishes are à la carte, with main courses at midday from about $4.00 and up; in the evening, from about $6.95 and up.

Open Sunday through Friday from noon until 10:30 p.m. (final order).

Closed Saturday, all major holidays and the last 2 weeks in August until Labor Day. Also closed for lunch on Sunday.

Reservations from 5:00 p.m. on required.

No credit cards.   PC

★★ PER BACCO!
140 East 27th Street   LE *2-8699*

Per Bacco! is the only restaurant we know that includes an exclamation point in its title, but it has more serious claims to distinction. The room, rather small, is charming, and you eat well from an extensive Italian menu.

We tried two pastas, both very good—cannelloni, at once full-bodied and delicate, and linguine al pesto.

Made with fresh basil when it is in season, this is one of our favorites when they use enough of the fragrant green leaves, and in this case they were generous.

Broiled shrimp with butter and garlic was top-notch, and baked clams very good. At the waiter's suggestion we tried liver sautéed with a touch of honey, which sounded odd at least, perhaps awful. He assured us it was delicious. It was.

Cocktails, wines and beer.

Complete luncheons are priced from about $4.75 to $5.50; table d'hôte dinners cost from about $5.75 to $9.00.

Open Monday through Saturday from noon until 10:00 p.m. Closed Sunday and all major holidays.

Reservations recommended.

AE   DC   MC

★★ PETER'S BACKYARD
64 West 10th Street   473-2400

This village steak house hasn't been around forever—only since 1905, serving ton after ton of high-quality beef cooked over an open charcoal pit in a non-stop picnic that is now counting its fans unto the fourth generation. That's mileage! There are also seafood specials.

Cocktails, wines and beer.

Open for dinner only with a special dinner at $10.95. A la carte dishes cost from about $5.25 to $12.50.

Open 7 days a week. Open Monday through Saturday from 4:30 p.m. until midnight; Sunday from 2:00 p.m. until midnight.

Reservations recommended.

Cocktail hour Monday through Friday 4:00 p.m. to 7:00 p.m.—all drinks $1.00.

AE   BA   CB   DC   MC

PIERRE AU TUNNEL, see AU TUNNEL

★★ PIETRO'S

201 East 45th Street   MU *2-9760*

Pietro's is just about as noisy as a restaurant can get, and so crowded that you have to sit elbow to elbow with strangers. The waiters, carrying on under difficulties, may seem brusque as you enter the small room from the narrow stairway leading to it, but they are only trying to avoid trampling you underfoot.

Everybody at Pietro's seems to know the people at several other tables; it is a restaurant of repeaters. And no wonder. The steaks are great, the pastas superb. The menu is incomplete (it lists nothing but spaghetti as pasta) and you had better ask for a little help in ordering. If you are not settling for steak, find out what the kitchen has on hand.

The great drawback is the crowding. If you happen to get next to a couple of argumentative strangers with loud voices and bad table manners, as has happened to us, you won't have much fun, but if you have better luck and are sympathetic to the sound of a crowded roomful of people talking and laughing, Pietro's can afford a great evening. Try to get a table by a window, which helps.

Cocktails, wines and beer.

Luncheon special $5.50 to $5.75; à la carte menu for lunch and dinner with entrées from $7.50 to $13.50.

Open Monday through Friday from noon until 10:30 p.m.

Closed Saturday and Sunday June through September; closed Sunday October through May.

Reservations required.

No credit cards.

206

★★ PIRO'S

1350 Madison Avenue (between 94 and 95 Streets)   *534-3016*

     With only 20 chairs, and some of the double tables occupied by singles and tables for four by couples, Piro's seldom accommodates more than a dozen or so diners at a time, and there's no place to wait except the sidewalk, so you're taking a chance. Better go with a second choice in mind somewhere in the area. If you get a table, a charming young woman will tell you what's available to eat that night and a chef who occasionally comes into the room to exchange badinage with the regulars will prepare your dishes individually. No mass preparation here. And it's very good. Ordinarily you'll have your choice of two or three pastas and chicken, veal, or shrimp prepared in whatever way the chef's mood prompts.

Wines.

Open for dinner only with table d'hôte prices from $8 to $10.00.

Open Tuesday through Saturday from 6:30 until 11:00 p.m.

Closed Sunday and Monday and the last 2 weeks in August.

Reservations recommended.

No credit cards

★★ P. J. CLARKE'S

915 Third Avenue (at 55th Street)   PL *9-1650 (front: 355-8857; back: 355-9307)*

     Putting P. J. Clarke's into a restaurant guide is like describing a roller coaster as a means of transportation. True, you can eat here, and eat well, but P. J.'s is first of all a combination mating ground, hip joint, extramural board room for advertising agencies, exposure area for theatrical and television hopefuls, and

207

just plain clubroom for a lot of handsome young people on the make in this, that, or the other field, who pack into the bar every night. Without having acquired the status of historical monument, P. J.'s is so famous and so revered that when all the surrounding buildings were torn down for a skyscraper, it was left standing in its old-fashioned crumbling brick integrity. You should at least poke your nose into this steamy purlieu. Bring your own sandwich in a brown paper bag, because chances are you'll never get through the mob at the bar to the dining room at the rear.

Cocktails, wines and beer.

A la carte entrées, throughout the day, cost from about $2.00 to $7.40.

Open 7 days a week from 11:30 a.m. until 4:00 a.m.

Reservations recommended at lunch, brunch and after-theatre; required at dinner.

No credit cards.

★★ PONTE'S STEAK HOUSE

39 Desbrosses Street   226-4621

From its out-of-the-way address near the docks, you'd expect Ponte's to be a rough little joint with a jolly chef-proprietor stirring a vat of spaghetti. Not so. Behind a modest entrance, this is an extravagantly plushy restaurant decorated largely in red, and so suggestive of a 1930's movie set that you expect Alice Faye to come in at any moment, all beads and feathers, to do her number. The place has in fact been used as a set for some recent movie or other requiring such a background.

In this rather eerie atmosphere the customers are prosperous, well-dressed, solid mind-your-own-business types. Instead of a menu, a blackboard on wheels is trundled around, and there are daily specials depending on the chef's choice from the markets nearby. Among standard items, we have found veal Marsala very tender and lavishly smothered in mushrooms, and veal Parmigiana worthy of its position as an Italian classic.

The restaurant will call a taxi for you if you need one on leaving. Otherwise, it's a walk of several blocks through dead streets. Odd place for a fancy restaurant.

Cocktails, wines and beer.

At lunch, table d'hôte is $4.95 to $8.95; complete dinner costs from about $5.50 to $10.95. Both are without appetizer.

Open Monday through Saturday from noon until 11:30 p.m.

Closed Sunday, New Year's Day, Washington's Birthday, Memorial Day, July 4th, Labor Day, Thanksgiving and Christmas.

Reservations recommended.

All major credit cards.

★★ PORTOFINO

206 Thompson Street   GR *3-9752 and 475-9241*

Anyone who has a nostalgia for Greenwich Village in the old days, or thinks he has one from acquaintance with paintings by John Sloan and other pictorial chroniclers of pre-Great Depression New York, will have a fine old time weeping into his spaghetti at Portofino. The three rather shabby rooms—let's hope they don't freshen them up—have a genuinely picturesque air with a clientele ranging from family groups to honest-to-goodness poets and painters, who somehow revert to ancestral type in a way that makes you wonder if the mysterious lady at that next table might be Edna St. Vincent Millay. We have found chicken portofino, boneless breast in a light sauce the best of the dishes we've tried here.

Cocktails, wines and beer.

Open for dinner only with à la carte dishes from about $2.50 to $4.25.

Open 7 days a week. Open Monday through Thursday from 4:00 p.m. until 11:30 p.m.; Friday, Saturday and Sunday until 12:30 a.m.

Reservations recommended.

AE   CB   DC   MC

★ PRESS BOX STEAKHOUSE

139 East 45th Street   986-4565

The menu includes fish, chicken, and various other dishes ranging beyond the typical steakhouse list, but the steaks are still the big thing here—in two senses of the word. The grilled sirloin for two people, charred black on the outside and just as you ask for it on the inside, with baked or french fried potatoes and a heap of excellent mixed salad included, would be hard to improve on as a meal of its kind. The atmosphere, neither elegant nor simple, is that of a slightly rundown businessman's pub. Phrasing that better: a slightly rundown pub for businessmen. But the ladies are welcome.

Cocktails, wines and beer.

A la carte entrées at lunch are from about $4.25 to $9.90; in the evening items cost from $6.95 to $12.50.

Open 7 days a week, except weekend lunch. Open Monday through Friday from 11:30 a.m. until 10:30 p.m.; Saturday from 4:00 p.m. until midnight; Sunday from 3:00 p.m. until 11:00 p.m.

Reservations recommended.

AE   BA   CB   MC   Schenleys, Exchange Media

★ PROOF OF THE PUDDING

First Avenue (at 64th Street).   *421-5440*

Proof of the Pudding is across the street from Maxwell's Plum, which is mighty tough competition, but the Pudding's sidewalk terrace, being somewhat less crowded, may have an edge on the Plum's as a spot for watching the picturesque pedestrian traffic of the neighborhood. The dining room is more than a bit kitsched up but the marble-topped tables are a pleasure. The chair backs for some reason have names painted in white, "Terrie and Al," or the like. Asked what it was all about, the maître d'hotel at one lunchtime said they were the names of customers who had died of food poisoning. Not so. The food is good and so is the service.

Cocktails, wines and beer.

A la carte entrées at lunch are from about $2.95 to $11.95. Table d'hôte dinner is $14.95 with à la carte items from $4.95 to $11.95. After 10:30 p.m., the menu is à la carte.

Open Sunday through Thursday from noon until 1:00 a.m.; Friday and Saturday until 2:00 a.m.

Reservations recommended.

Russian balalaika from 6:45 p.m. until closing on Monday through Saturday; piano on Sunday. Sidewalk terrace.

AE   BA   CB   DC   MC

★★ P. S. 77

355 Amsterdam Avenue (at 77th Street)   *873-6930*

Not a public school in spite of its odd name, this French restaurant is a relaxed spot where good cooking is served to a small but demanding clientele. Such dishes as snails in mushroom caps sauced with herb butter and garlic, or striped bass en papillote with herb and bacon topping, give you the idea. And not too expensive.

Cocktails, wines and beer.

A la carte entrées at lunch cost about $2.00 to $5.50. A la carte dinner dishes are from about $7.95 to $11.00, which includes salad and vegetable. Brunch items cost from $3.95 to $4.95.

Open 7 days a week from 11:30 a.m. until 11:00 p.m. Saturday and Sunday brunch is from noon until 3:00 p.m.

Closed the last week in August and Christmas and New Year's Day.

Reservations recommended at dinner.

AE BA MC

★★ PUERTA REAL

243 East 58th Street   758-9788

Everything about this small restaurant is attractive and the food usually lives up to the atmosphere. The chef specializes in Basque and Castilian cuisine and the service is marked by a flair for elegant Castilian manners. The only trouble is that when there is a crowd the very small kitchen has trouble keeping up with it, and one noisy party can shatter the peaceful air that otherwise sets Puerta Real apart from most restaurants its size.

When things are running well, the food is elegantly presented. Salpican de Mariscos, a seafood salad vinaigrette, comes so beautifully arranged on the plate that it seems a shame to eat it. Another excellent appetizer is called Pinchitos del Jefe Antonio, skewered veal and pork bits grilled to a fine crust.

There is an excellent—and very Spanish—chicken casserole with small onion, bacon, potatoes, and mushrooms in wine. Green salads, tossed with Spanish olives and onions, are first-rate.

212

Cocktails, wines and beer.

A la carte dishes at lunch are from $3.75 to $8.50. The à la carte menu at dinner is from $4.25 to $10.50.

Open Monday through Saturday from noon until 10:30; weekends until 11:30 p.m.

Closed Sunday and major holidays.

Reservations accepted at dinner.

AE   CB   DC

★★ PURBANI
1493 Third Avenue (between 84th and 85th Streets)
249-5016

This is one of the most attractively decorated Indian restaurants in the city, with a ceiling of Indian textiles, brass filigree lamps, and appropriate table ornaments. The food is good to excellent, with a lamb subjee—chunks of meat in a spinach sauce—among the best dishes. There is also a 16-course Indonesian dinner or rijsttafel that we tackled in part.

Purbani is not afraid of making spicy dishes as spicy as you would find them in India, but they will hold off on the hot stuff if you make it clear you're afraid of it. The lamb subjee mentioned above is normally a flavorful but not spicy dish, by the way. By all means get a side order of the chef's special chutney, a thin green paste fragrantly spiced that was new to us.

Tapes of traditional vocal and instrumental pieces complement the décor. For a change, they are sometimes played too low rather than too loud. Can't remember any other place where we've asked if the sound could be turned up.

Cocktails, wines and beer.

At lunch, à la carte dishes cost from about $2.25 to $2.75. Complete dinners cost $5.95 to $8.25, with à la carte items from about $3.95 to $5.95.

Open 7 days a week from noon until midnight.
Reservations recommended at dinner.
AE   BA

★   **QUO VADIS**
26 East 63rd Street   TE *8-0590*
This is still a handsome restaurant, but we haven't been too happy there recently. Service has been hectic and the food variable from indifferent to very good—which isn't good enough at the price. On our last (perhaps our final) visit we had to pour our own wine—oh, all right, how fussy can you get, but it is indicative of a lack of style—and were unable to catch the attention of the wine steward to order the second bottle we needed for our party. Never did get it. We had a good steak Diane, oversalted veal (the veal had been of high quality to begin with), and some very ordinary beginners and enders. At half the price, double the star.

Cocktails, wines and beer.
All dishes are à la carte, with main courses at midday from about $4.00 and up; in the evening, from about $8.50 and up.
Open from Monday through Saturday from noon until 11:00 p.m.
Closed Sunday and all major holidays. Also closed on Saturday during July and August.
Reservations recommended.
AE   CB   DC   MC

★★   **RENE PUJOL**
321 West 51st Street   *246-3023*
Thoroughly professional and well managed, this is a restaurant that respects the amenities of dining and can carry them out with skill, even if not with

brilliance. The chef seems to take special pride in the preparation of whatever he has chosen as the daily special, which is likely to be your best bet if you get there before it runs out.

At lunch we have been happy here with a simple omelette fines herbes, which may be elementary, but is still a test of a kitchen's efficiency when the restaurant is crowded.

Cocktails, wines and beer.

Table d'hôte at lunch starts at $5.50 and up; table d'hôte dinners cost about $8.25 to $10.25.

Open Monday through Saturday from noon until 11:00 p.m.; Saturday until 11:30 p.m.

Closed Sunday, 4th of July, Labor Day, Thanksgiving and Christmas.

Reservations recommended.

AE

★★★ RESIDENCE

1568 First Avenue (between 81st and 82nd Streets)
628-4100

Just keep the good news quiet and slip off to the Residence, which of all New York restaurants in its class must be the least widely known. It is not exactly inexpensive, but once you taste the food you may wonder why you aren't paying more, and why a table is ever available less than 48 hours in advance. From our six dinners there to date we would pick artichokes Lucullus (artichoke hearts topped by an excellent pâté) or mousse of either pike or sole as our favorite hors d'oeuvre. As entrées, well, any fish prepared in any way the restaurant wants, or orange duck, or paillard of beef or veal, or roast squab—or something picked blind off the rest of the menu. Service is excellent and the room is pleasant.

Cocktails, wines and beer.

All dishes are à la carte, with main courses at midday from about $5.50 to $8.00; in the evening, from about $7.75 to $11.50. Both include salad.

Open Monday through Saturday from noon until 11:00 p.m.

Closed Sunday, New Year's Day, July 4th, Thanksgiving and Christmas. Also closed the month of August until Labor Day.

Reservations accepted at lunch; required at dinner.

AE   BA

★★ REUN-THEP

860 Ninth Avenue (at 56th Street)   586-2240 and 586-8277

This is a really delightful little place with exquisite—I've chosen that word with care, by the dictionary's definitions of "carefully done . . . delicately wrought . . . keenly discriminating . . ." —cooking. People more familiar than we are with Thai cuisine assure us that it is authentic here. Authenticity makes less difference to us than the pleasure the end product gives us, and at Reun-thep that pleasure is great.

There are only 10 tables and we would like to protect them by saying that most of the dishes are quite spicy, by which we mean red-pepper-hot, which may keep a few explorers away. Ton Yom Khung (spicy shrimp soup) is a thin, lemony broth with delicious shrimp. Ga ro ti rin ham, translated as "tenderized half Bar-B Q chicken," wasn't exactly what we would call barbecued. Rather, it had been broiled, and was ravishing when dipped into the accompanying peppery sweet sauce. Nem nuong, "pork balls double cooked with oriental fine herbs" is accompanied by crisp vegetables encased in a light dough, offsetting in their coolness the extremely spicy pork balls.

The thing to do here if you are unfamiliar with Thai cuisine is to put yourself into the hands of the charming people who run this little place. You'll be beautifully taken care of and will taste things you probably haven't tasted before. Let me mention one more; cha kho is a fried whole fish simmered in a sauce of various herbs, and is delectable.

No liquor. Bring your own wine.

At lunch, the à la carte dishes begin at $2.95. Table d'hôte dinner is $6.95, with the à la carte menu from $2.95 to $6.95.

Open 7 days a week from noon until midnight.

Reservations accepted.

BA

★★★ RINCON DE ESPANA
226 Thompson Street   *475-9891*

Three stars, yes, but don't go to El Rincon de España expecting anything in the way of elegance. It's small, the tables are crowded, the service has about as much style as a wayside inn or a backstreet restaurant in a small Spanish city—and there's where the good things begin. In all except its literal geographical location this *is* a small restaurant in Spain, which is why it is always filled with aficionados of Spanish cuisine.

The food tends in general to be rather more spicy than the often bland Castilian cuisine that is most familiar in New York Spanish restaurants. The standard arroz con pollo (chicken with rice) isn't at all standard here; it is a casserole of chicken and sausage, country style, and the portion is gargantuan. Veal with almond sauce is prepared more along the conventional line and is exceptionally good. In addition to the almond flavoring, the sauce has a fruity taste something like apples.

Paella fans, which I am not, tell me that that dish is first-rate here. If you have the capacity to include an appetizer, the mejillones a la Carlos (mussels a la the chef here) are our first choice, in a peppery sauce. One order will do nicely for two. A flamenco guitarist, as genuine as the food, sometimes plays.

Cocktails, wines and beer.

The à la carte menu is priced from about $3.50 to $7.80, both for lunch and dinner.

Open 7 days a week from noon until midnight.

Closed Thanksgiving, Christmas and New Year's Day.

Reservations recommended at dinner.

All major credit cards.

★★ ROGER'S
324 East 57th Street   753-8270

This is a limited-menu steak-chops-and-fish type restaurant that moved from somewhere in the Hamptons and became a city boy. A very sophisticated bar, with piano, occupying a large balcony, gives the place a somewhat schizoid character, since the restaurant itself has retained some pseudo-dockside touches, a bit on the cute side.

A very good feature here is a special potato—mammoth chips that come to you still hot from the deep fry. The cooking in general has been good on our visits. Vegetables are treated with respect. Salads are bang-up. Among the more unusual dishes, calf's liver topped with avocado slices, an unlikely sounding combination, is excellent.

Cocktails, wines and beer.

218

Open for dinner only with à la carte entrées costing from about $7.50 to $11.00. Sunday brunch is prix fixe at $6.00, which includes one drink.

Open 7 days a week. Open Monday through Saturday from 6:00 p.m. until 11:30 p.m. Open Sunday from noon until 11:30, with brunch being served from noon until 3:00 p.m.

Closed during the summer.

Reservations required.

AE

★★ ROMEO SALTA

30 West 56th Street   246-5772

Here's a restaurant that is plainly in danger of coasting on its reputation. It must be included in a guide to New York dining because it is an elegant-looking place that has managed to retain an attractive clientele. But it puts us off from the beginning by charging $12.50 for a bottle of white Villa Antinori that sells at retail (the restaurant gets wholesale prices) at our corner liquor store for only $3.49.

Our latest lunch at Romeo Salta's: An escarole and bean soup, fine; prosciutto and melon, standard; fettucine Alfredo, average; scallopine of veal with lemon and butter sauce, just plain greasy—not oily or buttery, but greasy. This was true of the vegetable (zucchini) as well, although at least it wasn't overcooked. We finished with zabaglione, which was only fair, if you like it light, or quite good, if you like it thick. With tips, we spent $44 for a not very great lunch for two.

Why two stars? Because it's Romeo Salta's. It has a real air about it, and among the intangibles that you pay for, that's near the top.

Cocktails, wines and beer.

At lunch, table d'hôte costs from $9.50 to $11.50. The à

la carte dinner menu is priced from about $7.50 to $12.50.

Open Monday through Saturday from noon until 11:30 p.m.

Closed Sunday, Memorial Day, July 4th, Thanksgiving, Christmas, New Year's Eve and New Year's Day. Also closed the first 3 weeks in July.

Reservations recommended.

AE   CB   DC

★ ROSOFF'S

147 West 43rd Street   JU 2-3200

If it's "dining out" you're interested in, Rosoff's isn't likely to offer you all the amenities you expect, but a restaurant that has held its own for 75 years and is, in addition, convenient to the theatres, can't be omitted from this guide. Rosoff's makes up in copious portions and cheerful service whatever it lacks in elegance, which is fair enough.

Cocktails, wines and beer.

All dishes are à la carte, with main courses at midday from about $2.95 to $6.50; in the evening, from about $3.50 to $10.50.

Open 7 days a week. Open Sunday through Thursday from 11:30 a.m. until 9:00 p.m.; Friday until 11:00 p.m.; Saturday until midnight.

Closed Sundays during July and August.

Reservations accepted. Reduced parking from 5:30 p.m. until 6:00 a.m.: $1.50

AE   BA   CB   DC   MC

★★ RUC

312 East 72nd Street   RH 4-9185

Behind its narrow entrance, Ruc stretches back

through a surprisingly big room to an open garden that makes it half again as large in clement weather. Very little effort has been made toward picturesque effect—oh, a lamp post with a globe of colored glass in the garden, a few things like that—yet when you step in off 72nd Street there's a sensation of having dropped into one of the big, busy, inexpensive Czech or Hungarian restaurants from which this one— Czech—is descended. You feel, pleasantly, like a tourist who's had the luck to find a restaurant where the people you have shouldered in the street or on the bus come for a treat now and then. The American Express office is far away, although no doubt everybody has the credit card in their pockets.

Service, carried on by waiters in their shirtsleeves, ranging in age from about sixteen to seventy, is informal to the point of being abrupt, but your food gets on the table and the empty dishes get cleared away. True, your predecessors' cigarette butts may remain in the ash tray during your tenancy, but they won't mar too much your enjoyment of beef tenderloin with cream sauce, dumplings, and salad, or boiled beef with dill sauce and the same fixings, at a low price that has already included soup or juice and has dessert and coffee yet to come.

Cake for dessert turns out to be a cheap bakery product (we ate all of ours) and melon is a better choice. All told, not bad. Not bad at all.

Cocktails, wines and beer.

Open for dinner only, except weekends, with complete dinners costing from about $3.50 to $7.25.

Open 7 days a week. Monday through Thursday: 5:00 p.m. to 10:00 p.m. Saturday and Sunday: noon until 11:00 p.m. Friday: 5:00 p.m. until 11:00 p.m.

Reservations accepted.

From May through October the garden, seating 120 guests,
is open.

AE   CB   DC

★★ RUSKAY'S

323 Columbus Avenue (at 76th Street)   874-8391

Ruskay's is a restaurant that would revolution-
ize the business for the better if you could multiply
it by about 2000 in Manhattan. The kitchen operates
on a minimum menu changing from day to day that
assures proper attention to each dish while virtually
eliminating the waste that you pay for in the usual
restaurant.

The trick to this first-rate eating at low prices is that
you get a standard dinner (described on a card in the
window) that changes so often that you could board
at the place with pleasure. One day the menu will
begin with marinated asparagus in onion and tomato
sauce (the asparagus very crisp and the sauce thin,
fresh, and slightly spicy), and go on to an entrée of
breast of chicken with a delicate cheese sauce, green
beans cooked just right as your vegetable, and a generous salad of chicory, lettuce, and tender young
arugula.

Breads are rather special. One day it will be a twist
a friend identified for us as "challa," and another time,
a fresh-baked small loaf. Desserts run to excellent pas-
tries.

The hitch is that you can't get into Ruskay's unless
you go very early or hit a very slow night. (Just try.)
There's no space for waiting inside, the whole place
being given over to tables and a counter given over
to serving meals, not drinks.

222

The décor is chastely art deco except for a pressed metal ceiling preserved from some earlier day, with ceiling fans that really operate. In the best of all possible worlds, everybody would live next door to a Ruskay's.

Wines and beer.

All dishes are prix fixe. Hot lunch is $3.00; chef's salad is $2.00. Dinner is $8.00. Saturday and Sunday brunch is $4.00. After-theatre special supper is $6.00. All prices include sales tax.

Open 7 days a week from noon until midnight. Saturday brunch is from noon until 4:00 p.m.; Sunday brunch is from noon until 3:30 p.m.

No reservations
No credit cards.

★★ RUSSIAN TEA ROOM
150 West 57th Street   CO 5-0947

What the Union of Soviet Socialist Republics needs, according to our memory of restaurants there on a recent trip, is a few Russian Tea Rooms. "Tea room" this isn't, but a full-fledged restaurant where borscht with sour cream, blinis with red caviar—or black if you own a couple of gold mines—beef Stroganoff, dilled meatballs, and other Russian specialties along with American dishes have been served up hour after hour, day after day, year after year, decade after decade, with a consistency and equanimity of culinary détente that should set an inspiring example for our politicians. But maybe it's easier in the kitchen.

The Russian Tea Room is practically next door to Carnegie Hall, a before-or-after-the-concert place, popular with performers as well as audiences.

Cocktails, wines and beer.

A la carte entrées at lunch cost from about $5.25 to $6.50, which includes dessert and beverage. Table d'hôte dinner is from about $7.75 to $12.75, with à la carte entrées priced from about $5.25 to $12.25. After-theatre à la carte dishes are from $3.75 to $12.25.

Open 7 days a week. Open Sunday through Friday from 11:30 a.m. until 1:00 a.m., 2:00 a.m. on Saturday. Sunday brunch is from noon until 3:00 p.m.

Reservations recommended.

AE   BA   DC   MC   Schenley's

★★★   SAITO

305 East 46th Street   759-8897

There is also a Saito restaurant at 8 East 49th Street (telephone 758-3114) but the diminutive Saito-San topped her own record when she opened this larger and fancier branch. There's everything you want here, from a tempura bar to a special tempura counter available for parties, plus tatami rooms where Westerners can sit on the floor but have a convenient well under the table where their legs can hang down—a compromise arrangement now familiar in Japan also. Just think of it not as a cop-out, but a tribute to the length of American legs rather than the rustiness of your joints.

Saito is Westernized to the extent that it has the glossy cosmopolitan air of a big Tokyo restaurant, but the food and service can be as authentically Japanese as you want it. If you make a point of telling them—in advance for a really bang-up party—that you're not afraid of anything and that they can shoot the Japanese works, you'll have a meal that is bounteous and so beautifully prepared that it is as effective pictorially as gastronomically. For the timorous or uninitiated, the menu is explicit enough in its descriptions to let you know in advance whether you are going to be attracted, puzzled, or terrified by what you find on your plate.

The service at Saito is exemplary.

Cocktails, wines, beer and sake.

All dishes are table d'hôte with luncheons costing from about $4.00 to $10.00; in the evening, prices are from $10 to $20.00.

Open 7 days a week. Open from Monday through Friday from noon until 10:00 p.m.; Saturday and Sunday from 5:00 p.m. until 10:30 p.m.

Closed Saturday and Sunday for lunch and all major holidays.

Reservations recommended.

AE CB DC MC

★★★ SAL ANTHONY'S

55 Irving Place (between 17th and 18th Streets)   982-9030

On a recent visit to Sal Anthony's we took a friend to lunch upon his return from Rome and Naples where, he said, he hadn't had a decent meal for two weeks. Whatever the explanation of that unprecedented experience, he found Sal Anthony's pasta and shrimps arreganata what he had been looking for without success in their home territory. This is really an excellent Italian restaurant, both as to food and ambiance. A fine bay window at the front looks out onto a red brick building across the street that will remind you of what a comfortable place New York used to be, if you knew it about a generation ago.

Cocktails, wines and beer.

All dishes are à la carte, with main courses at midday from about $3.25 to $5.75; in the evening, from about $4.25 to $9.00.

Open 7 days a week from 11:30 a.m. until midnight.
Reservations recommended.
All major credit cards.

★★★ SARDI'S
234 West 44th Street   221-8440

Sardi's, New York's living legend as the one, the only, the great theatrical restaurant, could serve empty plates without losing its clientele. The walls are lined with signed caricatures of Broadway personalities from away back and on up to the current hits, hung frame to frame. The same celebrities turn up at the tables from time to time but if you are a celebrity-hunter you might be disappointed, since the majority of the big names among the diners will be producers, writers, public relations people, agents, and others whose faces don't get into the limelight like those of the actors whose careers they make.

Lunch on matinee days should be avoided at Sardi's, but it is the perfect restaurant for dinner before going to one of the cluster of theatres nearby. (A reservation is imperative.) Food? Sardi-goers will tell you it isn't all that good, but this is a reverse manifestation of affection. Eggs Benedict, deviled beef bones, a violent garlic-laden cannelloni, and chicken à la Sardi, which is slices, mostly breast, on a bed of asparagus, covered with cream sauce, and put under the broiler—all these are good.

Because most people want a table downstairs, Sardi's serves the same food upstairs for smaller prices with outsize cocktails as another lure. Many regulars have begun going up there. The upstairs bar is an especially good spot for lingering over a couple of drinks.

Cocktails, wines and beer.

The à la carte menu at lunch and dinner is priced from about $3.95 to $13.00.

Open from Monday through Saturday from 11:30 a.m. until midnight.

Reservations recommended.

AE   BA   CB   DC   MC

★★ SAZERAC HOUSE

533 Hudson Street   989-0313

The building, dating from 1826, is designated as an historical landmark by the City of New York but the jukebox is strictly of the moment. You won't be thrown out if you turn up in a coat and tie, but you may feel conspicuous. As the name indicates, Sazerac House takes its cue from New Orleans. In addition to Sazerac cocktails at the bar, there are approximations of various Creole shrimp dishes that are about as close as you can get without fresh Louisiana shrimp, a flounder Pontchartrain (on a bed of spinach in a light cream and cheese sauce) that is excellent, and a hefty bowl of jambalaya that's beyond criticism. Service is good, the atmosphere warm and friendly—but the noise is something else when juke's on the loose.

Cocktails, wines and beer.

All dishes are à la carte, with main courses at midday and brunch from about $1.50 to $3.95; in the evening from about $3.95 to $5.75.

Open 7 days a week from noon until midnight. Saturday and Sunday brunch is from noon until 4:00 p.m.

Closed Thanksgiving and Christmas.

Reservations recommended for dinner.

AE   BA   DC   MC

★★ SCOOP

210 East 43rd Street   MU *2-4483*

A visit to Scoop is recommended. The food is good to excellent (pushing up toward a third star), the service is efficient and friendly, the general air of the place is bright, even festive, and the prices aren't all that high as prices go in good midtown New York restaurants. Among other nice touches, tiny pizzas are likely to come with your drinks, and a bottle of anisette is customarily placed on the table along with your espresso. Whatever you order, be sure to ask for french-fried zucchini (if in season). Scoop's is the best we have tasted anywhere.

The menu lists pastas in half portions, which is sensible. We have tried beef, veal, chicken, fish, and seafood here, and there's not much chance that you will be disappointed in any of them. The atmosphere is lively rather than intimate, and the name, rather odd for an Italian restaurant, is a reference to the high percentage of reporters and other newspaper people among the clientele.

Cocktails, wines and beer.

All dishes are à la carte, with main courses at midday from about $4 to $9.50; in the evening, from about $4.50 to $11.50.

Open Monday through Saturday from noon until 11:00 p.m.

Closed Sunday, July 4th, Labor Day, Thanksgiving, Christmas and New Year's Day.

Reservations required at lunch and recommended for dinner.

Free parking from 5:30 p.m. until 1:00 a.m.

AE DC MC

★★ SEAFARE OF THE AEGEAN
25 West 56th Street   LT *1-0540*

The wide-ranging menu in this enormous restaurant includes not only the Greek preparations indicated by its name, but a list of Creole specialties and a Bombay curry as well as the standard dishes you expect in any American fish house. As a first and imperative virtue—the fish is fresh as can be. As a second, the quarters have not accumulated the ingrained fishy aura that comes faintly even to some of the best seafood restaurants as time goes by. Also, this is a real restaurant with tablecloths and all that—not one of those pseudo-dockside jobs. All to the good. However, we found the preparation better than average but not great, and the service, while cheerful, was anything but efficient.

Cocktails, wines and beer.

Special luncheon is from about $6.25 and up, which includes soup and coffee. The à la carte menu is also available for lunch. A la carte entrées at dinner are priced from $6.95 and up.

Open 7 days a week. Open Monday through Saturday from noon until 11:00 p.m. Open Sunday from 1:00 p.m. until 11:00 p.m.

Closed Thanksgiving, Christmas and New Year's Day.

Reservations accepted.

All major credit cards.

★★ SHINBASHI
280 Park Avenue (entrance on 48th Street)   *661-3915*

In décor this may be New York's prettiest Japanese restaurant, with sophisticated simplifications of traditional Japanese interior design crossbred to good effect with the slick abbreviations of neo-Bauhaus.

There are tatami rooms if you feel like sitting on the floor. If you don't, there are tables overlooking a beautifully raked pebble garden.

We had bad luck with the "Japanese formal dinner, selected by our Chef," which comes (at prices current at this writing) at $20 or $30 per person. The food was simply piled up in front of us instead of being served in gracious courses. Make sure ahead of time that you will get it properly presented in courses over a nice long evening and it should be satisfactory, for the food is good, often prepared with ingredients hard to come by outside Japan.

Cocktails, wines, beer and sake.

Table d'hôte at lunch is from $4.25 to $15; à la carte dishes are from $6 to $10. Table d'hôte dinners are from $5.90 to $30; à la carte entrées from $5.90 to $11.00.

Open Monday through Friday from noon until 10:00 p.m.; Saturday from 5:30 p.m. until 10:00 p.m.

Closed Saturday for lunch, all day Sunday and major holidays.

Reservations recommended

Private ozashiki as well as western tables and chairs available.

AE CB DC MC

★ SHUN LEE DYNASTY

900 Second Avenue (at 48th Street)   PL 5-3900-1-2

Along with the standard roster of Chinese dishes you'll find some unusual concoctions here—so unusual that they are unheard of in China. There's a spicy calf's liver, for instance. Portions are enormous and the cooking is satisfactory, but on our latest visit, made for the purpose of checking up on this formerly highly rated favorite, we felt that most of the sparkle

had gone out of the kitchen along with a certain tar-
nishing of the glittery décor. Still, however, an acceptable Chinese restaurant with the fillip of the chef's
inventions.

Cocktails, wines and beer.

*All dishes are à la carte, with main courses at midday from
about $2.50 to $4.75. In the evening the à la carte menu is
priced at about $10.75, tax included.*

*Open 7 days a week. Open Sunday through Thursday from
11:30 a.m. until 11:30 p.m.; Friday and Saturday until 1:00
a.m.*

Closed Thanksgiving.

Reservations recommended.

AE   CB   DC

★ **SIGN OF THE DOVE**
1110 Third Avenue   UN *1-8080*

With its grillwork, gas lamps, and garden, the
Sign of the Dove looks like a brand-new New Orleans
restaurant decorated in pseudo-French Quarter style
for the tourist trade—which doesn't mean that it isn't
very pretty indeed. It also attracts handsome young
people who serve as paying ornaments. The food
doesn't live up to the décor and the clientele, but it
is quite acceptable. There's many a restaurant where
you eat better but enjoy it less.

Cocktails, wines and beer.

*All dishes are à la carte, with main courses at midday and
brunch from about $5.95 to $10.95; in the evening, from about
$7.50 to $12.50.*

*Open 7 days a week except Monday lunch. Open Tuesday
through Thursday from noon until midnight; Friday and
Saturday until 1:00 a.m. Open Monday from 5:30 p.m. until
midnight. Saturday brunch is from noon until 3:00 p.m.;*

Sunday brunch is from noon until 4:00 p.m.
Closed for Monday lunch.
Reservations recommended.
Sidewalk cafe and open courtyard dining. Pianist at lunch and brunch. Piano nitely in bar. Tuesday through Saturday evenings piano and violin.
Reservations recommended.
AE BA CB DC MC

★ SIXISH

1701 First Avenue (at 88th Street)   722-6161

We give Sixish a star with a bit of reluctance and with the warning that it is a disharmonious double-header of a raffish bar with a screaming jukebox in one half, and a homey little restaurant, eager to please, in the other. Unfortunately the noise of the first half carries over into the second. The jukebox is apparently stocked with a selection of numbers called "Music To Get Indigestion By," and if the barflies aren't keeping it going, the management is.

In the restaurant you find good scone-like bread waiting for you in a warmer at your table and a short list of inexpensive wines available as accompaniment to such daily specials as roast beef (an enormous portion) with a baked potato, sour cream, green beans with almonds, and a fresh salad of lettuce, tomato, and green pepper. With similar accompaniments we found that striped bass with dilled Hollandaise was an excellent dinner. Service is friendly, prices are low, and the atmosphere (for the deaf) cozy.

Cocktails, wines and beer.

A la carte dishes at lunch are from about $1.50 to $7.95. At dinner, the à la carte menu is from $3.95 to $8.50, which includes salad, vegetable and potato. Sunday brunch is $3.95, *which includes a Bloody Mary or sangría. The snack after-theatre menu is from $1.75 to $5.75.*

Open 7 days a week from 11:30 a.m. until midnight; snacks until 2:00 a.m. Sunday brunch is from noon until 4:00 p.m.

Closed the Friday before Labor Day until the following Thursday. Also closed Christmas, New Year's Day, Easter, Memorial Day and the 4th of July.

Reservations accepted.

Live minstrel or piano Monday through Saturday from 9:00 p.m. until 1:00 a.m. Art exhibit changes every 2 months.

AE   BA   DC   MC

★★ SPRING GARDEN (HOUSE OF SIAM)
2596 Broadway (at 98th Street)   749-4524 or 864-9016

Formerly a Chinese restaurant, House of Siam is now a hybrid, with Thai food predominating. Something not to be missed here are the hors d'oeuvre of beef slices and chicken chunks cooked on small braziers at your table and eaten with a sweet and spicy peanut sauce. You might follow this with mussels in a delectable broth tasting of lemons and herbs before going into the entrées, where your multiple choices include chicken with ginger; shrimp with spicy tomato sauce or with garlic; beef with oyster sauce, snow peas, and mushrooms; and whatever else the waiter suggests. If you have a party of four or six or more, the opportunities for exploration are legion.

There's no liquor license and we didn't spot a liquor store nearby, so it's safest to bring your own. Arriving at the address you may think you have gone wrong, but you haven't. The restaurant is on the second floor, up a stair reached through an inconspicuous doorway.

No liquor. Bring your own wine.

A la carte dishes at lunch are from about $2.95 to $5.95.

The dinner à la carte menu is from $3.95 to $7.95.
  Open 7 days a week from 11:30 until 12:30 a.m.
  Reservations accepted.
  Thai costume dancers nightly.
  AE

★ SUERKEN'S

27 Park Place   CO 7-6389

Although Suerken's can't vie with Miller's (which see) as the occupant of an architectural landmark, it does occupy engagingly picturesque quarters in the City Hall area. Behind the rather ratty remains of a fine old cast-iron façade, the interior is a mangled but still pleasant period piece with a few iron columns left, a really fine old bar, and some rotating electric fans that are beginning to look as picturesque as the ceiling variety that have become antiques.

In addition to the steak-and-chops menu favored around City Hall, Suerken's has a good, if not exactly imaginative, chicken pie. Service is casual and friendly, and the atmosphere altogether relaxed.

  Cocktails, wines and beer.
  A la carte dishes at lunch and dinner cost from about $2.50 to $8.00.
  Open Monday through Friday from 11:00 a.m. until 8:00 p.m.
  Closed Saturday and Sunday.
  Reservations accepted.
  Party and banquet facilities available for up to 100 guests.
  AE BA CB DC MC

★ SUN LUCK EAST CHINESE AMERICAN RESTAURANT

75 East 55th Street   PL 3-4930

★ SUN LUCK IMPERIAL
935 Lexington Avenue   LE *5-4070*

★ SUN LUCK TIMES SQUARE
200 West 44th Street   *524-4707*

Food at all the Sun Luck restaurants is modified to please American taste, but being large enterprises, they are consistent in the quality of this food because less subject to the tantrums and departures of chefs that plague smaller Chinese restaurants not family-run. Of the four, Sun Luck Imperial is the most elaborately decorated and has particularly good facilities for large parties, and Sun Luck Times Square is—appropriately for the area—the gaudiest.

Cocktails, wines and beer.

Table d'hôte lunches are from about $2.50 to $4.75. The à la carte dinner menu is from $3.00 to $8.50.

Open 7 days a week from noon until 1:00 a.m.

Reservations recommended at lunch.

Private party facilities available at each branch.

AE   CB   DC   MC

★ SUN LUCK WEST
157 West 49th Street   *582-8182*

★ SZECHUAN D'OR
243 East 40th Street   *683-4411*

This is a comfortable, amiable, leisurely Chinese restaurant that hits a level somewhere between the big, gaudy ones looking like Shanghai brothels out of an old George Bancroft movie that are typical uptown, or the stark, crowded little rooms that serve the best food in Chinatown. "Szechuan" is supposed to

235

mean spicy food, but it seldom does in New York. As in other Chinese restaurants catering to American palates, the waiters at Szechuan d'Or can't bring themselves to take you at your word when you say you want a dish really spicy, and it isn't the same when you have to add at the table a few dollops of liquid fire—red peppers ground in oil—that should have gone into the making in the kitchen. But otherwise, this is a very pleasant small Chinese restaurant, family style, with well-prepared standard dishes.

Cocktails, wines and beer.

The à la carte menu at both lunch and dinner is priced from about $1.95 to $6.50.

Open 7 days a week from 11:30 a.m. until 11:20 p.m.

Reservations accepted.

AE MC

★ **SZECHUAN IMPERIAL**
228 East 45th Street   867-3070

Atmospherically this new Chinese restaurant must be the most curious in New York—unintentionally. Taking over the quarters of an Italian restaurant that folded, the management left the crimson plush, the brass central chandelier and some rather awful brass bacchanalian low reliefs, and added red-tasseled Chinese light fixtures and some quite good Chinese calligraphic wall panels. Add to all this the variety of programs selected on the radio. On one evening these ranged from a Schumann concerto to the sound track of a television program on hyenas in the wild. The food? Well above average, and the Taiwanese chef longs to prepare special dishes in advance.

Cocktails, wines and beer.

236

A la carte entrées at lunch and dinner are from $2.75 to $8.50.

Open 7 days a week from 11:30 a.m. until 11:30 p.m.
Reservations accepted.
AE DC

★★★ TANDOOR
40 East 49th Street   752-3334

Tandoori specialties (dishes prepared in the clay oven known as a tandoor) are normally on the mild side, and if you want your Indian food hot, you'll have to insist on it. But if you like the flavor of Indian food with the spice toned down, you'll be happy with it as it comes.

Tandoor makes a great point of its rumali chapati, a bread made of whole wheat dough flattened out to a diaphanous disk and cooked over a clay mold, a real tour de force of technique. From time to time during the evening, the chefs, behind a glass window, put on a display of their skills. Worth watching.

Tandoor is the handsomest ethnic restaurant in New York, combining a kind of metropolitan crispness with lush Indian references. Service is good. Be sure to ask for the mint chutney.

Cocktails, wines and beer.

Lunch is $4.50, with buffet lunch prices at $4.95. A la carte entrées at dinner are from $1.50 to $5.00, with table d'hôte dinner costing from $6.50 to $7.00.

Open 7 days a week, except Sunday lunch, from 11:30 a.m. to 10:30 p.m.

Closed for Sunday lunch and all major holidays.

Reservations recommended.

AE BA DC MC

★★ TANPOPO

139 East 52nd Street   935-9241

Very small, but never hectic even when very full (which is the rule at lunch), this is one of the pleasantest Japanese restaurants of its size. We found the dipping sauce for the tempura more than usually delightful in flavor, and the scallions rolled in beef and grilled couldn't have been improved on.

Cocktails, wines, beer and sake.

Complete lunch is from $4.95 to $5.95, with à la carte dishes from $3.85 to $5.95. The à la carte dinner menu is from about $2.75 to $5.50, with table d'hôte dinners from $6.95 to $8.25.

Open 7 days a week except Saturday and Sunday lunch. Open Monday through Friday from noon until 10:30 p.m.; Saturday and Sunday from 5:00 p.m. until 10:30 p.m.

Closed Saturday and Sunday lunch. Also closed New Year's Day, Memorial Day weekend, Independence Day weekend, Labor Day weekend, Thanksgiving, and Christmas.

Reservations recommended at lunch; accepted at dinner.

AE DC MC

★★ TOKUBEI

1425 Second Avenue (between 74th and 75th Streets)
288-5470

This is an unpretentious little partially Westernized Japanese restaurant run by a group of young people in T-shirts. You can find very much the same kind of restaurant in Tokyo or even Kyoto these days—a kind of Japanese bistro.

Things are nicely presented here. The sashimi (four kinds of raw fish) is offered on its own traditional wooden miniature table, the thin slices interleaved with slices of lemon and cucumber. There's enough in a single order to make a good first course divided

238

for two people, which the restaurant does cheerfully. We found that Tokubei's vegetable tempura, again divided, made a delightful second course. Whatever cooked fish they are offering is likely to make a fine entrée; the restaurant apparently observes the admirable Japanese passion for preparing only the freshest possible. But we also liked very much the chicken teriyaki, grilled with soy sauce.

The first impression is of extreme simplicity, but there are some really good Japanese prints on the walls and attention to other nice details, once you start looking. It's a very agreeable spot.

Cocktails, wines, beer and sake.

Open for dinner only, with à la carte dishes from about $3.25 to $7.95. Table d'hôte dinner is from $5.50 to $9.95.

Open Tuesday through Sunday from 5:30 p.m. until midnight.

Closed Monday.

No reservations.

AE MC

★ **TONY'S ITALIAN KITCHEN**
212 West 79th Street   874-9017
My records show that a couple of days before Christmas, 1974, four healthy adults and two small boys who were too tired to do more than dawdle with half-portions of spaghetti and meat sauce, all got out of Tony's Italian Kitchen for only $53 including tax, tip, wine, and more glasses of milk than I was able to count. Without recalling individual dishes, I remember that everybody got fed, that everything tasted good (we might have been in a large, inexpensive, popular restaurant almost anywhere in Italy between Milan and Sicily), and that the service, including

cheerful acceptance of the kiddies, was friendly.

It's a bright and shiny restaurant, wasting no money on fancy decorations or other refinements of dining. But for just plain eating, it does very well indeed.

Cocktails, wines and beer.

At lunch, à la carte dishes cost from about $3.15 and up. Dinner table d'hôte is from $7.75 and up.

Open 7 days a week from noon until midnight.

Closed Christmas.

Reservations recommended.

Party and banquet facilities available for 10 to 60 guests. AE DC MC

★ **TORREMOLINOS**

230 East 51st Street (between Second and Third Avenues) 755-1862

Torremolinos goes in heavily for Spanish atmosphere and could easily be a restaurant catering to tourists in Madrid or Seville. There is a fake arcade, a fake fireplace, and fake beams, one of which cuts across the room several feet below the ceiling as a perch for a collection of copper pots, luster plates, and a big air conditioner. The entire staff is Spanish, and you may find a flamenco guitarist and singer at dinner.

We have had variable experiences at Torremolinos—some mediocre food at lunch, and one excellent dinner when we were served a fine mixed salad, a really delicious peppery seafood soup, a beautifully grilled sole, good tournedos, and instead of dessert a "coffee Torremolinos," which is a rich, sweet mixture of coffee, brandy, whipped cream, and spices.

There was a $10 overcharge on the check, which we

noticed just in time. Accidents, of course, will happen, even in the best of restaurants. But they shouldn't.

Cocktails, wines and beer.

All dishes are à la carte, with main courses at midday from about $3.50 to $8.50; in the evening from $5.95 to $9.95.

Open from Monday through Thursday from noon until 11:00 p.m.; Friday and Saturday until midnight.

Closed Sunday.

Reservations accepted.

AE CB DC MC

★ TRE AMICI

1294 Third Avenue (between 74 and 75th Streets)   *535-3416*

Here's a fairly large, densely decorated, vigorously Italian restaurant with some pretensions to style that don't come off and a kitchen that turns out good food. You might call the cuisine either hearty or rough, depending on how much subtlety you demand of straightforward Italian dishes. There's a lot of tomato sauce and cheese. The ingredients are good, and the portions more than generous, as a rule. Service is attentive and the customers, to judge by this restaurant's popularity, love everything.

Cocktails, wines and beer.

Open for dinner only with à la carte dishes from $4.00 to $11.50.

Open 7 days a week. Open Sunday through Thursday from 5:00 p.m. until 1:00 a.m.; Friday and Saturday until 2:00 a.m.

Closed Thanksgiving, Christmas and New Year's Day.

Reservations recommended.

Piano bar in lounge area nitely. Customers can select lobsters from lobster tank.

AE CB DC MC

★ **"21"**

21 West 52nd Street   582-7200

Unless they know you at "21" there's not much point in trying to get in, and there's not much point in getting in if you're not already known once you're inside. Except by formal definition this is not a restaurant but a club, and you're not going to be happy there unless you're a member in good standing. It's as simple as that. The kitchen and the ambiance for the regulars is easily three-star. The restaurant's policy toward the general public is minus-two. Let's settle for one. It won't make any difference to "21," which has been a roaring success since Prohibition, when there were special reasons for its selective policy.

Cocktails, wines and beer.

All dishes are à la carte, with entrées at midday from about $7.50 to $12.50; in the evening, from about $11.00 to $17.50. The after-theatre special supper menu is from $12.00 to $18.50.

Open Monday through Saturday, except summer, from noon until 12:30 a.m.

Closed Sunday, New Year's Day, July 4th, Labor Day and Christmas. Also closed on Saturday from May until September.

Reservations required.

AE CB DC MC

★★★ **UNCLE TAI'S HUNAN YUAN**

10-59 Third Avenue (at 62nd Street)   TE *8-0850*

With a menu that includes rabbit dishes (orange rabbit among them) and wild game in season, along with specialties unique to the house as well as standard fare, Uncle Tai's must be the most inventive Chinese kitchen in New York. The room is large, the tables generously spaced, and an army of captains and waiters provide excellent service. We'd prefer not to be handed our check while finishing our last cups of tea for the implied accommodation of people waiting to be seated, but otherwise no complaints and much praise.

Cocktails, wines and beer.

All dishes are à la carte, with main courses at midday from $3.50 and up; in the evening, from about $5.25 to $14.50.

Open 7 days a week. Open Sunday through Thursday from noon until 11:00 p.m.; Friday and Saturday until 11:30 p.m.

Reservations recommended.

AE   DC

★★ VASATA

339 East 75th Street   650-1686 or 650-1422

At the risk of creating an international incident, we have to say that if there are any important differences between Hungarian and Czechoslovak cuisines they have escaped us. Vašata, however, is emphatically Czechoslovak by declaration. It's a bright, clean, happy place where you will find first-rate duck, roast pork, chicken paprika, and schnitzels. A pleasant aspect of Vašata is that the waiters seem to enjoy their jobs.

Cocktails, wines and beer.

Open for dinner only, except Sunday, with table d'hôte dinner from about $4.55 to $10.95 (one dollar less for entrée only).

Open 7 days a week. Monday from 5:00 to 10:00 p.m.; Tuesday to Saturday from 5:00 to 11:00 p.m.; Sunday noon until 10:00 p.m.

Closed the last 2 weeks in July.

Reservations recommended.

AE   MC

★★ XOCHITL

146 West 46th Street   PL *7-1325*

Some people say that Xochitl (pronounced So-sheetl, with most of the "t" swallowed) is the best Mexican restaurant in New York, and we will string along so far as the flavor and authenticity of its few dishes are concerned, but let's admit that they are very few, and very unadventurous. The attitude of the management seems to be that if you've been in the same location for 40 years, pleasing people and making money, why change the status quo? They've got a point. They've also got low prices.

The place is unpretentious, with rather uncomfortable booths along the walls at either side of a row of small tables down the center of a narrow room—definitely not a place to sit around and enjoy the atmosphere, but you are well taken care of. About one thing there's no question: Xochitl does have the best tortillas in town. Mexican food buffs have learned to pick them up regularly (ordering in advance) to take home. (They need reheating by steaming, or by dipping in hot oil just until soft, depending on how you plan to use them.)

Also, Xochitl is in the theatre district and service is fast enough to help you get to your show as the curtain goes up.

Cocktails, wines and beer.

The à la carte menu is priced from about $3.00 to $4.00 for lunch. A la carte entrées at dinner are from $4 to $6.00.

Open Monday through Saturday from noon until 10:00 p.m.

Closed Sunday, Thanksgiving and Christmas.

No reservations.

No credit cards.

★★ YOSHI'S

52 West 55th Street   *265-8141*

This very attractive little restaurant calls its cuisine "Japanese continental," with steaks, roast beef, roast chicken, grilled pork, beef Stroganoff, salmon steak, sea food au gratin, and french fries representing the mysterious West on a dinner menu dominated by such familiar Orientalia as teriyaki, sukiyaki, tempura, sushi, and sashimi. Connoisseurs of Japanese food will miss the more elaborate dishes available at larger, more purely Japanese restaurants, but everything at Yoshi's is excellently prepared, beautifully presented, and true enough to Japanese tradition. One warning: the wines are poor, and it is best to stick to sake, which comes in a pretty little bottle, properly warmed.

Among the entrées, the beef dish called negimaki is so good at Yoshi's that it should be listed as the house specialty. Thin strips of beef, broiled on one side and very rare on the other, are wrapped around a core of fresh green scallions. Very pretty to look at and a joy to eat. Another good beef dish is yakiniku, marinated and broiled.

Two people having dinner can have these as entrées after beginning with yakitori (barbecued chicken on skewers) and a small order of sashimi (raw fish) as shared appetizers, going on to a second course of a shared order of mixed tempura (shrimp, fish, and vegetables deep-fried in batter), and then the entrées, making it clear to the waiter that you want the courses one at a time. We like to end a Japanese meal with soup. The one called suimono is fine at Yoshi's, a delicate, clear broth with a lemony tang.

Cocktails, wines, beer and sake.

All dishes are à la carte, with main courses at midday

from about $4 to $6; in the evening, from about $4.50 to $6.50.

Open Monday through Saturday from noon until 10:00 p.m.

Closed Sunday, Christmas and New Year's Day.

Reservations recommended.

AE   DC   MC

★★ YUNNAN YUAN

144 East 52nd Street   PL 9-8260

This is a good Chinese restaurant under the usual drop-in circumstances. Honey-cured ham, abalone, squab soup, and Szechuan roast duck are at the top of one epicure's list. But the kitchen is at its best when put to the challenge of arranging a banquet for, say, eight or ten people, with the chef given free rein to serve what he pleases. We attended one of these as the guest of a Chinese friend, and although we couldn't give you the name of a single dish, it was superb from beginning to end. Visiting Yunnan Yuan on other occasions we have noticed that there is usually a banquet going on for Chinese diners—a corroboration, always, of a Chinese restaurant's high quality.

Cocktails, wines and beer.

The à la carte items at lunch cost from about $3.50 to $3.95; in the evening, from about $3.50 to $6.75.

Open 7 days a week from 11:45 a.m. until 11:00 p.m.

Reservations required at lunch; recommended at dinner.

AE

★★★ **Z**

117 East 15th Street   *254-0960*

The food at Z is hard to beat in the tradition of hearty popular Greek fare served in portions that seem to take for granted that you haven't eaten for a couple of days and don't expect to eat for a couple following. There are no frills here as to décor, elegant service, or subtle preparation. It's just straight down the line good Greek cooking for its own sake, and it is greeted when it arrives at table with a gusto that is a tribute to the capacity of the human stomach to accommodate itself to unreasonable demands. And in comparison with most New York restaurant prices, Z gives the food away. The prices account for Z's third star, since we try to average them in with the quality, the ambiance, and other such factors.

You'll find the everyday classic Greek dishes excellent here. Among the somewhat less familiar ones, arni spanaki is a mountainous joint of lamb with sautéed spinach tasting of a spice—maybe cinnamon, maybe nutmeg. Also there's exochico, chunks of lamb with Greek cheese and vegetables baked in a pastry casing. But maybe, all told, moussaka remains the best Greek bet, and it is as good at Z as it is in Greece.

Wines and beer.

A la carte dishes at lunch are from about $1.80 to $3.65. Dishes at dinner are from $3 to $3.95 and include salad, coffee and dessert.

Open Tuesday through Friday from 11:30 a.m. until 11:30 p.m. Saturday and Sunday from 1:00 p.m. until 11:30 p.m.

Closed Monday, Thanksgiving and Christmas.

No reservations.

No credit cards.

247

★★ ZAPATA'S

330 East 53rd Street   *752-9738*

This is a really good restaurant, small and over-crowded but worth whatever juggling you have to do to arrange your schedule for a day and hour (early) when you are most likely to be able to squeeze in. It gets its second star on the basis of a valiant effort to approximate a classic mole verde, which is moderately successful, and the fact that it offers cabrito—kid—on occasion, usually weekends. If you want it, better telephone first to find out when you can get it. Zapata's calls it "baby goat."

Always having been fond of cabrito, but familiar with it only as a grilled or barbecued meat, we were surprised to find it served at Zapata's as a black stew best described as a cross between boeuf bourguignon and civet de lapin. (Cabrito bourguignon? Civet de cabrito?) The meat is very tender, slightly gamey in flavor, and Zapata's sauce is moderately violent. A large portion comes, like other main dishes, with beans and rice.

All ingredients at Zapata's are high quality. The ground meat in the chiles rellenos makes them a superior version of the standard. "Swiss enchiladas," as they call them, are chicken served with a fresh sauce of tomatoes and peppers.

Among the hors d'oeuvre, the ceviche—in this case very fresh sweet shrimp in a bath of lime juice with raw onions and herbs—is a delight. For a bit of crisp green stuff with onions and peppers, add napolitos—baby cactus salad.

About every five minutes at Zapata's you are all but blasted out of the place by a ventilator that goes on without gale warning. Don't worry. It always goes off again, and it's nice to be able to breathe.

Cocktails, wines and beer.

All dishes are à la carte, with main courses at midday from about $2.95 to $3.95; in the evening, from about $4.75 to $7.25.

Open 7 days a week from noon until 11:30 p.m.

Closed Thanksgiving and Christmas.

No reservations.

AE   MC